Cost, Use, and Value

COST, USE, AND VALUE

The Evaluation of Performance, Structure, and Prices across Time, Space, and Economic Systems

FRANCIS SETON

with a special Annex contributed by

Dr Albert E. Steenge

CLARENDON PRESS · OXFORD

1985

Oxford University Press, Walton Street, Oxford OX2 6DP
Oxford New York Toronto
Delhi Bombay Calcutta Madras Karachi
Kuala Lumpur Singapore Hong Kong Tokyo
Nairobi Dar es Salaam Cape Town
Melbourne Auckland
and associated companies in
Beirut Berlin Ibadan Mexico City Nicosia

Oxford is a trade mark of Oxford University Press

Published in the United States
by Oxford University Press, New York

British Library Cataloguing in Publication Data
Seton, Francis
Cost, use and value: the evaluation of performance, structure and prices across, time, space and economic systems.
1. Value
I. Title
338.5'21 HB201

ISBN 0-19-828471-3

Library of Congress Cataloging in Publication Data
Seton, Francis.
Cost, use and value.

Bibliography: p.
Includes index.
1. Prices. 2. Value. 3. Comparative economics.
I. Title.
HB221.S418 1985 338.5'2 85-259
ISBN 0-19-828471-3

Typeset at the Alden Press Oxford London and Northampton
Printed in Great Britain by
Biddles Ltd, Guildford

To My Wife

PREFACE

Unassuming titles make unread books – ambitious titles, disappointing ones. I may have promised too much. But let the reader take forewarning by paying the subtitle of this book the same attention as the opening fanfare; for it expresses the original intention: to conduct a modest exercise in the much-maligned economics of comparative systems analysis, which only gradually revealed itself as an application of the conceptual synthesis through which the notion and measure of 'value' emerges from the two opposite poles of cost and utility. It is, indeed, little more than an illustration of this synthesis, one among several methods of achieving it; but even this may go some way towards justifying the main title of this book.

It would have been fascinating, and no doubt equally valuable, to trace the *Ideengeschichte* of this synthesis from the early toying with simple ratios through the selection of common loci uniting functional relationships, to saddle points, fixed-point theorems, and all the sophisticated tools of latter-day mathematicians who have not played their last card in this game (and probably never will). Such, however, goes well beyond my intention, and vastly beyond my capacity. Like an untutored child in a sequential question-and-answer game, I prefer to start out from simple perplexities as they reveal themselves in the attempt to grapple with concrete issues, e.g. the comparability of ratios internal to different economies, and to be led step by step into the more abstract realm by the manifest deficiencies of the obvious answers prompted by a series of questions of gradually increasing difficulty.

The opening chapters of Part I of this book are designed to introduce the problem of inter-system and inter-country comparability in simple form and to outline the desiderata of a possible solution in numerical terms, without the use of algebra. From Chapter 6 onwards a general solution is approached in abstract terms starting from the cost and utility sides in turn, and culminating in the proposed convergence of these approaches in the concept of 'eigenprices'. In the process the reader is introduced to the newly devised 'accent notation' which may cause practitioners of the art of linear algebra some passing discomfort. I venture to assert, however, that the initial effort will be quickly overcome and amply repaid in terms of ease of application in paper and pencil work, general transparence, economy of symbols, and lack of ambiguity. The notation is introduced in n. 1 of Chapter 6 and repeated for ease of reference in Appendix 1, which also contains a directory of the most commonly used symbols in the book. Readers who have difficulty with the algebra should be able to refer back to the numerical treatment in earlier chapters to convince themselves that the solutions sought and suggested are indeed those corresponding to the desiderata displayed in the arithmetic examples.

It may be appropriate at this point to emphasize that, as far as this book is concerned, I claim no originality for the use of dominant eigenvalues as a way of finding fixed points in linear transformations and thereby forming the desired synthesis underlying the concept of 'value'. This approach has by now a history covering twenty years or more, in which the author may claim to have played a modest part (see n. 5 of Chapter 10). The novelty, if novelty there be, lies rather in the particular choice of the matrices that serve as the basis for these eigenvalues, their definition, derivation, and interpretation.

Part II is an attempt to elucidate the nature of eigenprices and eigenyield by establishing links with older established and more widely known economic concepts, some of which may be presented as the result of eigenprice calculations in highly simplified or 'degenerate' systems. Readers should find Chapters 14, 15, 18, and 22 of particular help here, but should take special warning from Chapters 23–25. The remaining chapters of Part II, particularly Chapters 16–18, are extensions of the method which, in the attempt to throw a bridge to marginal analysis, introduce additional complications, but may remain unread without prejudice to the understanding of the basic issues.

The empirical exercises of Part III, as will be repeatedly stated in the text, are added as mere illustrations of where the method will lead when applied to the rough-hewn and ill-adapted data that official statistics has at present on offer. A proper application to data specially collected and tailored to the purpose in hand, which alone could yield reliable results, would require a research effort far beyond the scope of this book or our unaided resources. The tentative results of Part III are therefore no more than a 'game with figures' to ascertain whether meaningful and superficially plausible results emerge. This caveat applies with less force to the Special Annex contributed by Dr Steenge than to the pilot survey undertaken by myself. However that may be, the outcome of both exercises gives reason to hope that a further, more intensive, research effort would be well worth while, and that the new concepts introduced in this book could play a part in pushing back the frontiers of our knowledge of the world's economies.

My indebtedness to colleagues in the profession, both senior and junior, is profound and varied in scope. Dr A. E. Steenge, the contributor of the Special Annex, paid me the compliment of choosing an earlier article I had written on the subject as the starting point for his own independent researches on Holland and Hungary, and thus provided much of the encouragement without which this book might never have been written. Distinguished colleagues at home and abroad were good enough to listen to or read summary versions of it in seminar or article form, and declared themselves interested, intrigued, puzzled, critical, or hostile, but never – except in one (anonymous) instance – in a mood to be dismissive. Among those who made invaluable comments were Professors P. A. Samuelson, P. J. D. Wiles, M. Morishima, and J. A. Mirrlees, Messrs T. Gorman and M. FG. Scott of Nuffield College, Oxford, Professor K. Laski of the University of Linz, Mr S. Gomulka of the London School of Economics, and Dr Gy. Szakolcsai of the Econometrics Institute of the Hungarian Academy of Sciences. A different, but hardly less profound, debt of gratitude is due to those who put their outstanding computing skills at my disposal – Mr Colin Carpenter of Bradford University and his assistants; Giuseppe Mazzarino of the Oxford University of Economics and Statistics, and Mr Erik Dietzenbacher of the University of Groningen, all of whom acquitted themselves of an unenviable task with good humour and consummate skill. I alone, however, remain responsible for errors and misconceptions and for the sheer presumption of launching a book on a subject in which so much unfinished business still remains to be done.

Last, but not least, I wish to record my gratitude to my personal secretary and Chief Secretary of Nuffield College, Miss Jean Brotherhood, who coped with the typing of a complicated and sometimes confused manuscript with patience, good humour, and attention to detail far beyond the call of duty.

Nuffield College, Oxford F. S.
July 1984

CONTENTS

PART I

Eigenprices: Definition and Characteristics

1 Introduction 3
2 The challenge of comparability 6
3 'Cost-fetishism' – monomania versus pluralism 12
4 'Use-fetishism' 18
5 Eigenprices 22
6 The basic scheme in algebraic terms 25
7 The 'full-cost pricing' of commodities – valuation by cost 29
8 The 'full-price costing' of factors – valuation by use 32
9 Alternative interpretations of 'use-norms' 35
10 Eigenprices and derivatives – definition and algebra 41
11 Eigencost and eigenyield 44
12 The 'scaling' of eigenprices 50
13 A method for generating eigen-prices and cost ratios 52

PART II

Eigenprices: Historical Parallels, Special Cases, and Extensions

14 The production of commodities by means of primary factors only ('feedback-free' models) 57
15 The link with marginal analysis – a linear programming approach 60
16 The link with marginal analysis – the Principle of Reciprocal Marginality generalized 63
17 The link with marginal analysis – a detailed application of the PRM to two-by-two models 66

18 The production of commodities by means of commodities only ('factor-free' models) 76
19 'Partial' eigenprices – specific uses 79
20 OECD shadow prices for project appraisal 82
21 'Partial' eigenprices – specific factors 89
22 'Marxian labour values 91
23 Eigenprices – a summary of basic characteristics 96
24 Eigenprices – possible uses 98
25 Caveats 101

PART III

Eigenprices: A Foray into the Real World

26 Introduction 107

IIIa A Pilot Survey of Eigenprices from Cross-section Data 109
27 The data 109
28 The problem of aggregation 113
29 Price-deviance and eigen-yield 116
30 Measured eigenprices and current pricing behaviour 121
31 Structural eigenratios 125
32 Further experiments with eigenprices 127

IIIb Time-series Analysis for the Netherlands and Hungary (Special Annex contributed by Dr A. E. Steenge) 129
33 Introduction 129
34 Brief characterization of the postwar Dutch economy 133
35 Eigenprices for the Netherlands, 1948–78 137
36 Discussion of the results for the Netherlands 143
37 A brief characterization of postwar Hungary 146
38 Empirical results for Hungary, 1970–79 150
39 Discussion of the results for Hungary 158
40 Concluding remarks 161

APPENDICES

Appendix A – Notation and directory of symbols 163
Appendix B – Eigenprices and cost-values 169
Appendix C – The current and standardized eigen-structure of the United Kingdom in 1972 173

Index 177

LIST OF STATISTICAL TABLES (PART III)

Ten Economies in Descending Order of 'Price Deviance'

Ten Economies in Descending Order of Eigenyield

Eigenprices and Current Pricing

Cases of Substantial 'Overpricing'

Structural Eigenratios in Various Economies

Sectoral Eigenprices for the Netherlands, 1948–78

Eigenprices of Primary Factors and Eigenyield for the Netherlands, 1948–78

The GNP by Origin, Netherlands, 1948–78

The GNP by Factor Share and Final Use, Netherlands

Hungarian Eigenprices for 18 Macro-sectors (on standard factor-base)

Hungarian Eigenprices for 18 Macro-sectors (on reduced factor-base)

Hungarian Eigenprices for 9 Macro-sectors

Hungarian Eigenprices for 5 Macro-sectors

PART I

Eigenprices: Definition and Characteristics

1
INTRODUCTION

It is well-known to the point of notoriety that economics can never be an experimental science. The phenomena and relationships that the economist observes are not embedded in an environment that can be varied at will to isolate particular actions or reactions; he must forever find his way in a world where every effect remains assignable to diverse causes, and every cause is fraught with multifarious effects. Thus frustrated in his vying for honours with physicists, chemists, or biologists, he had to seek solace in a different aspiration – that of achieving at least the status of an *exact* science, a body of systematic knowledge operating with concepts, aggregates, or variables which are defined to allow the largest possible number of logical relationships to be deduced between them, giving maximal scope for valid prediction in a world of uncertainty, and spelling out the fullest possible implications of the choice between disposable means towards given ends or between competing ends within reach of available means. To the extent that this has been successful, it has been achieved by stripping economic reality down to bare essential: a faceless assembly of factor-owners and 'economic men', the proverbial single factory, or even a single machine with interlocking parts – a 'black box' into which are fed primary resources ('factors') at one end to be transformed into final commodities ('goods') at the other for the use of consumers, investors, or public policy-makers. The black box vision is now so ingrained in the minds of quantitative economists that even the traditional notions of cost, utility, and value – overlaid with atavistic impurities though they still are – have taken on formal meanings little different from mathematical functions, derivatives, mappings, or transforms on specially defined domains, with nothing left for thick lips to kiss or heavy boots to kick.

It should be stated from the outset that this book takes its stand on the black box vision, not because its author believes that there is nothing to be explained outside it, but because he feels that the analysis to which it has given rise has been, and continues to be, one-sided in several important respects, and that some of its potential for generalization still remains to be explored. In particular, the backward linkage, which relates final goods to primary factors, the process of costing, has seldom been logically matched in thoroughness and emphasis by the forward linkage, relating factors to final goods through which the factors could be evaluated or 'normed' according to their ultimate productivity or *usefulness*; and the concept of *value* with which most economists operate (outside the rarified Paretian world of universal optimization) still fails to synthesize the twin ingredients of *cost* and *use* in an even-handed manner and remains tainted with an ingrained bias of 'cost-fetishism'.

With so much unfinished business still to be tackled in the conceptual sphere, we may be forgiven for side-stepping a number of well-known and probably unresolvable conundrums attaching to the black box vision, such as the separate measurability of inputs and outputs (e.g. 'capital' and 'profit') or the criteria for the division between them (e.g., is 'work ethics' an *input* or *output* of the system, or merely part of the environment in which the system operated?). We beg leave to brush such stumbling blocks aside, in order to focus on the central question: How can the physical flows and proportions of specified inputs and outputs be compared in rationally commensurable terms to produce internally consistent and valid criteria of economic structure and performance, consonant with established notions of cost, use, and value, and amenable to international and inter-systemic comparison without imparting biases inherent in a country-specific, time-specific, or arbitrarily chosen price structure?

This comparability across time, space, and different economic systems is in our view the litmus test for the general validity of the value-concept or 'standard of value' that is being applied. The value of, say, a ton of coal may need to be assigned vastly different numbers of units, in countries with profoundly different cost conditions and economic needs such as Britain and China. We may not even be able to express it in commensurable units, and the same may be true of each and every commodity entering the national income. Yet if comparison between gross national products (GNPs) and their structural characteristics are to be possible at all, there must exist some methodologically uniform value-concept applicable to both countries whose adequacy to each environment and freedom from bias can be universally accepted. Conversely, a value-concept, however satisfying on philosophical, logical, or mathematical grounds, will never command universal credibility unless it permits direct intertemporal, international, and intersystemic comparisons of greater validity than country-specific or arbitrarily chosen price systems. Validity entails comparability, and comparability attests validity. It is for this reason that we put intersystemic comparison at the centre of this book, even though its basic objective is the wider one of exploring economic concepts and placing traditionally accepted valuation systems in the context of the wider family to which we believe them all to belong.

2
THE CHALLENGE OF COMPARABILITY

Questions of the comparative size, growth, structure, or performance of different economies have for long dogged economic analysts as well as policy-makers and the common man. It is scarcely possible to decide on, or justify, crucial measures in the field of commercial, investment, or defence policy without giving credence to some such statements as 'The USA spends under 7 per cent of its GNP on defence[1] while the USSR spends over 14 per cent',[2] or 'For every unit absorbed in household consumption the Soviet Union spends twice as much on capital investment as the United States',[3] etc., etc.

It does not take much persuading to make the purveyors of such information choke on their own words. The ratios being compared are clearly and crucially dependent on the prices in which the underlying aggregates are valued. Those of the West are – in principle at least – derived from the interplay of market forces, transformed or distorted by random concentrations of monopoly power, fiscal policy, tariff protection, etc. Those of the Soviet Union derive from the edicts of central authorities acting under historical, ideological, or administrative constraints and unhampered by an overriding need to use prices for market-clearing – a function that can be safely left to queuing, residual foreign trade, or direct administrative intervention. This being so, the defence share or investment ratio in GNP can be made to appear whatever the planners wish, and juxtaposition with the corresponding Western statistics makes about as much sense as comparing a bootlace with a piece of string. Yet the human mind lusts for comparisons of just that kind, and few statistics carry any meaning to economists unless they can be compared in their different manifestations in space and time. Can we devise a method, crystal, or prism through which they can be viewed in these different guises without losing the assurance that we are still looking at the same thing?

It is this hope that launches us on the quest for an unbiased price system in terms of which physically heterogeneous inputs and yields can be made commendable – a quest that has produced a number of holy grails in the past, and an even larger host of knights-errant. In this book we propose to add to their number, but, instead of setting out from the famous round table of King Arthur, we shall take our starting point from the even more famous Square Table of King Wassily (Leontief). Our indebtedness to illustrious 'knights of the Square Table' like, Sraffa, Morishima and others, will become abundantly clear in what follows. But we hope to go beyond them and, in particular, to attempt to lay the twin ghosts of 'cost-fetishism' and 'monomania' which have frightened off so many who might otherwise have rallied to their banner.

Before the exorcism can begin, however, we need to pay our respects to the scholarship and ingenuity that has gone into previous attempts to circumnavigate the reefs thrown up by differently based price systems in the way of those who wished to make meaningful comparisons between different systems or to compile valid league-tables of various sorts. To our mind these attempts can be brought under three main heads, and it might be as well to pass these in review, however summarily.

'Price-pruning'

Professor A. Bergson, the pioneer and past-master of the art of inter-system comparisons, originally put his faith in what might be called 'price-pruning', the careful pruning of conceptually empty or non-comparable prices of their extra-economic incubus in the hope of reducing them to a better reflection of each country's own internal factor-costs. His 'adjusted factor cost standard' forms the basis of the classical series of estimates of the Soviet national income and product (SNIP),[4] which for the past three decades have so insistently and persuasively invited comparison with its US and generally Western counterparts.

The method has found distinguished followers, and an impressive literature of comparative assessment has now sprung up.[5] Its sources, apart from Professor Bergson himself, were earlier attempts to come to grips with the problem of differential or distorted prices, often in a slightly different and sometimes dynamic, rather than static, context.[6] Naturally there has been no lack of doubters and critics,[7] and the notion that, even with ostensibly free labour markets, a reduction to internal factor costs would solve the comparability problem has been subjected to severe and and to our mind quite damaging criticism.

'Price-grafting'

An even more popular method of seeking comparability takes its cue from the statistical methodology of index numbers, and revalues the economic aggregates of one country systematically in the prices of another, in order to measure the results against the unadjusted data of the latter. The method could probably trace its ancestry as far back as the computation of 'standardized' mortality rates or rates of incidence of disease, crime, etc., designed to eliminate the distorting effects of differential age or class structures on the crude figures, or to the construction of output indices of the Laspeyres or Paasche type, which value commodity flows of different time periods in the constant prices of the initial or the final year. From this it is only a short step to the use of 'neutral' price systems imported from third countries, intermediate years, or 'the world as a whole', a universal valuation system which has found its most complete expression in the United Nations' International Comparison Project (ICP).[8] Although this particular exercise was concerned primarily with the comparison of costs and purchasing power, the method has also been used to compile league tables of GNP, GNP per head, and the main components of final demand.

In all cases, the method suffers from an inescapable ambiguity, as the results of comparing countries A and B normally give sharply different, and often conflicting, verdicts according to which of the two countries is chosen to furnish the uniform price basis. It may be concluded that such 'transplants' of organically alien valuations can at best eliminate the bias arising from *differential* pricing, but cannot escape the residual bias inherent in any one country- or time-specific price structure *per se.* When such hybridization between two countries is replaced by recourse to a common standard alien to both by drawing on the price structure of a third, supposedly 'neutral', country, the choice of that country introduces additional degrees of freedom into the result, which commands confidence only to the extent that arbitrariness is accepted as a substitute for neutrality. To cast the 'world as a whole' in the role of the third country appears to inject an element of objectivity by restricting arbitrary choice, but hides other assumptions of doubtful validity, such as the notion that the appropriateness of a country's price system as a universal yardstick is proportional to its size, population, prosperity, or whatever furnishes the weight with which it figures as a constituent of 'the world' in international statistics.

On a more theoretical level, the use of Laspeyres-, Paasche-, or Geary-type ICP indexes can be justified as an approximation to a postulated single family of indifference curves representative of all countries involved, allowed to differ from each other only in the particular region of the indifference map they happen to offer for empirical observation. The Kravis–Gilbert method of taking geometric means would then be tantamount to fitting a homogeneous-quadratic family to the regional slopes detected in this manner[9] and accepting this construct as the 'substratum of common humanity' to which the idiosyncracies of every nation can trace their origin. Attractive though this notion is, the eye of healthy scepticism will see in it no more than a sophisticated form of statistical wishful thinking whereby unrevealed truth can be discovered by concocting suitably recondite averages from revealed falsehoods.

'Price-cloning'

With this fanciful expression we push our horticultural analogy to a risky limit (the phonetic affinity with the verb 'clowning' will surely not be lost on our critics) to characterize the method of using a single concept to generate family groups of country- and time-specific price systems 'in the womb' of each of the economies to be compared, thus producing universal indicators – evaluated not by a uniform yardstick which cannot exist, but by a uniform principle which can find application in widely different contexts.

To some extent this is also the approach implicit in Bergson's 'adjusted factor-costs'. Historically, however, it has made its greatest impact with the emergence of what we have elsewhere called 'diagnostic' prices[10] – prices whose role is neither *descriptive* (of actual exchanges anywhere in time or space) nor *functional* (in the sense of pushing the economy towards an optimum, however conceived), but 'investigative', probing for hidden truths, 'unmasking' or 'exposing'. It is our purpose in this book to develop this notion to its limit and to propose a new system of diagnostic prices for inter-system comparison designed to overcome the main objections that have been levelled, rightly, against earlier representatives of the species, such as the Marxian 'labour values'.

Let us, however, review these objections and explore the ways in which they invalidate the claims to justice or veracity that are advanced.

Notes

1 The figure for 1970–5 was estimated at 6.6 per cent; see Joint Economic Committee, Congress of the United States, *East European Economist Post-Helsinki*, US Government Printing Office, Washington, 1977, p. 274.

2 The figure is implied by the CIA estimate of 40–45 billion rubles on Soviet defence spending (including R & D) for 1970 and official data for Soviet (GNP 285.5 billion roubles in 1970); see Joint Economic Committee, Congress of the United States, *Soviet Economy in a New Perspective*, US Government Printing Office, Washington, 1976, and Ts. S. U. *Narodnoe khozyaystvo SSSR v 1980 g.*, Finansy i Statistika, Moscow, 1981, p. 380.

3 Abram Bergson, *The Real Income of Soviet Russia since 1928*, Harvard University Press, Cambridge, Mass., 1961, p. 277.

4 Abram Bergson, 'Ruble Prices and the Valuation Problem', *Quarterly Journal of Economics*, August 1950; *Soviet National Income and Product in 1937*, Columbia University Press, New York, 1953; Abram Bergson and Hans Heymann Jr, *Soviet National Income and Product 1940–48*, Columbia University Press, New York, 1954; Abram Bergson, *The Real National Income of Soviet Russia since 1928*, Harvard University Press, Cambridge, Mass., 1961.

5 Oleg Hoeffding and Nancy Nimitz, *Soviet National Income and Product 1949–55*, RAND Corporation RM-2101, April 1959; Abraham S. Becker, *Soviet National Income 1958–1964*, University of California Press, Berkeley and Los Angeles, 1969 (for a discussion of the valuation problem see Part I, Chapter 3, p. 43 *et seq.*

6 Naum Jasny, 'Intricacies of Russian National Income Indices', *Journal of Political Economy*, August 1947; Alexander Gerschenkron, 'The Soviet Indices of Industrial Production', *Review of Economic Statistics*, November 1947; Donald Hodgman, *Soviet Industrial Production 1928–1951*, Harvard University Press, Cambridge, Mass., 1954.

7 P. Wiles, 'Are Adjusted Rubles Rational?', *Soviet Studies*, October 1955; F. D. Holzman, 'The Adjusted Factor Cost Standard of Measuring National Income: Comment', *Soviet Studies*, July 1957.

8 Methods and procedures are fully set out in Irving B. Kravis, Zoltan Kenessy, Alan Heston, and Robert Summers, *A System of International Comparisons of Gross Product and Purchasing Power*, Johns Hopkins University Press, Baltimore, 1975.

9 I am indebted to Professor Samuelson for pointing this out to me.

10 Francis Seton, 'The Question of Ideological Obstacles to Rational Price Setting in Communist Countries', in Alan Abouchar (ed.), *The Socialist Price Mechanism*, Duke University Press, Durham, North Carolina, 1977.

3
'COST-FETISHISM' – MONOMANIA VERSUS PLURALISM

3a Labour monomania

This beguiling obsession finds its obvious justification in the Marxist ideology which identifies a single production factor, 'homogeneous labour', as the sole fount of all economic benefit and imputes to it the totality of all 'value' residing in goods and services.[1]

This labour-value, more appropriately labelled 'full labour-cost', is thus defined as the sum-total of homogeneous labour[2] absorbed in a unit of a commodity, whether contributed *directly* in the workshops that turn it out or *indirectly* as 'embodied' in the materials, fuels, etc., expended by these workshops in its making.

Contrary to an earlier impression among economists, including some of outstanding distinction, we believe that the Marxian notion, however one-sided and inadequate as a measure of what we normally conceive to be 'value', has a clear operational meaning; in fact, it can be given unambiguous quantitative expression by following well-defined computational procedures in any economic system composed of a finite number of sectors or 'industries' (each producing a single commodity with the aid of other commodities, labour, and other factors), provided only that the inter-sector flows are measurable in independent physical or quasi-physical units. A three-sector scheme expressed in such units might be a suitable illustration (see Table 3.1).

In the absence of price discrimination, which we shall assume throughout, the physical units used are replaceable by current money-values, say 'goods-lira-worths' or 'goods-liras' (glr), to be regarded as surrogates for a composite physical unit, which side-step the issue of homogeneity by allowing variations in quality or micro-mix to be 'homogenized' through current-price weighting. Similarly, factor

Table 3.1

	Coal industry	Power industry	Service industry
Commodity inputs			
Coal	160 tons	20 tons	60 tons
Electric power	100 kwh	125 kwh	125 kwh
Services	–	–	–
Factor inputs			
Capital	£6 worth	£18 worth	£6 worth
Labour	78 hours	54 hours	34 hours
	↓	↓	↓
Outputs	300 tons coal	450 kwh power	£255 worth services

inputs could be measured in 'factor-liras' (flr) with the same objective, while keeping this factor unit dimensionally distinct from the goods unit (glr). Within the compass of goods-lira we must of course distinguish 'coal-liras' (clr) from 'power-liras' (plr) and 'service-liras' (slr), while factor-liras may be either 'capital-liras' (clr) or 'labour-liras' (llr). Indeed, tedious though it may seem, we can avoid the risk of 'dimensional incoherence', which is ever-present in exercises of this sort, only by spelling out the dimension of every value we use (i.e. providing it with its proper unit) whenever it occurs.[3]

In terms of the newly introduced 'homogenized' units, our scheme might take on the form presented in Table 3.2. By subtracting the sum of the three sectoral inputs in each row from the corresponding output figures, we find that the GNP (final list of commodities) consists of the aggregate shown in the last column.

If a unit lira of every commodity were measured by its proper 'labour-volume' (in terms of labour-liras), this would result in a revalued

Table 3.2

	Coal industry	Power industry	Service industry	Final uses (GNP)
Commodity inputs				
Coal	80 clr	10 clr	30 clr	30 clr
Power	20 plr	25 plr	25 plr	20 clr
Services	–	–	10 slr*	75 slr*
Factor inputs				
Capital	6 klr	18 klr	6 klr	–
Labour	39 llr	27 llr	17 llr	–
Outputs	150 clr	90 plr	85 slr*	

*Services, as the product of the third industry, are classified as commodities and therefore measured in liras (slr).

scheme in which the first three input columns must sum to the 'indirect labour cost' of the three outputs which, when added to the unchanged 'direct labour cost' (fifth row), must give the properly revalued outputs of the last row. It is clear that one and only one set of three values (multiplicative coefficients) will achieve this result, namely the values 0.70, 0.52, and 0.68, which have the dimension flr/glr. Applying these values (and rounding) our scheme changes into that of Table 3.3. In this scheme the contribution of capital is completely excluded from the formation of output values – as is the intention of the Marxist doctrine – and the latter are unequivocally and wholly attributed to labour.

It is clear that a change in any of the three coefficients (0.70, 0.52, and 0.68) would destroy this identity – either by opening up a gap between the sum of direct and indirect labour costs and the labour-value of outputs, thus leaving part of the latter for attribution to some factor other than labour, or by causing the latter to fall short of the former, thus failing to account for all the labour expended in the value of the commodity. In either case the changed coefficients could no longer be regarded as expressions of the true Marxian labour-values, which are therefore uniquely and adequately measured by the three coefficients above.

This completes our illustrative example of the characteristics of the full labour-costs and the – so far only intuitive – demonstration of their existence and characteristics. In a later chapter we shall offer a general method for their computation by means of linear algebra.

Table 3.3

	Coal industry	Power industry	Service industry
Commodity inputs			
Coal	56 llr	7 llr	21 llr
Power	10 llr	13 llr	13 llr
Services	–	–	7 llr
Indirect labour costs	66 llr	20 llr	41 llr
Direct labour cost	39 llr	27 llr	17 llr
Full labour cost	105 llr	47 llr	58 llr

3b Capital monomania

It is clear by analogy from the argument above that we could with equal ease derive 'full capital costs' for the three commodities – a set of value coefficients that would impute their total values to the capital

Table 3.4

	Coal industry	Power industry	Service industry
Commodity inputs			
Coal	14 klr	2 klr	5 klr
Power	6 klr	8 klr	8 klr
Services	–	–	3 klr
Indirect capital costs	20 klr	10 klr	16 klr
Direct capital costs	6 klr	18 klr	6 klr
Full capital costs	26 klr	28 klr	22 klr

inputs in the fourth row of Table 3.2. These coefficients turn out to be 0.17, 0.30, and 0.25 klr/glr for the three commodities respectively, resulting in the revaluation shown in Table 3.4.

Again, the sum of the revealed indirect and direct capital costs yields the original output revalued in the same system. This time, however, it is labour, not capital, that is excluded from any part in value formation. Table 3.4 demonstrates that the set 0.17, 0.30, and 0.25 klr/lr is indeed the set of full capital costs per unit and that no variation in any of them could be made without destroying the defining identities.

3c Composite factor-costs

So far we have been able to derive commodity valuations only in terms of *alternative* single-factor costs, such as the capital-costs in klr/glr and labour-costs in llr/glr shown in the first and second rows of the 'cost-matrix':

$$\begin{pmatrix} 0.17 & 0.30 & 0.25 \\ 0.70 & 0.52 & 0.68 \end{pmatrix}$$

'Monomaniac cost-valuations' of this sort can of course give us as many commodity costings as there are factors of production, but they cannot furnish any criteria for the choice between them. Short of any doctrine or ideology that would determine such a choice, we can obtain a *single* costing for our commodities only by imputing relative weights or 'norms' to the separate factors, purportedly measuring their scarcity, utility, or any other index of preference that could be applied to them. Such a weighting, say (f_1, f_2), would allow us to express the 'total direct factor inputs' in rows 4 and 5 of Table 3.2 in commensurable units (factor-lira) as the 'composite factor' absorption by the coal industry ($6f_1 + 39f_2$), the power industry ($18f_1 + 27f_2$) and the service industry ($6f_1 + 17f_2$). This would obviously result in commodity costings measured by a similar weighting of the rows of the cost matrix above, i.e.

$$0.17f_1 + 0.70f_2, 0.30f_1 + 0.52f_2, \text{ and } 0.25f_1 + 0.68f_2$$

for the three commodities (all expressed in flr/glr). Thus, if labour were weighted twice as heavily as capital, the full composite factor-costs of commodities would be 1.57, 1.73, and 1.61 flr/glr, corresponding to direct factor inputs of 84, 72, and 40 respectively (Table 3.2).

To bring our costings into conformity with the traditional notion of 'full costs', we shall in addition assume that they include a uniform mark-up of $\sigma = \left(\frac{1}{\phi} - 1\right)$% on material and factor-costs, where ϕ is the uniform 'cost/turnover ratio', thus converting our full-cost matrix to

$$\frac{1}{\phi}\begin{pmatrix} 0.17 & 0.30 & 0.25 \\ 0.70 & 0.52 & 0.68 \end{pmatrix} \tag{3.1}$$

and the corporate full costs of commodities to

$$\frac{1}{\phi}(0.17f_1 + 0.70f_2), \frac{1}{\phi}(0.30f_1 + 0.52f_2), \text{ and } \frac{1}{\phi}(0.25f_1 + 0.68f_2). \tag{3.2}$$

Clearly, therefore, under a 'pluralist' system of valuation, the full costs of commodities must be (linearly) dependent on the 'factor-norms' (f_1, f_2), for whose assessment we do not so far possess any rational criteria, and this is as far as 'cost-fetishism' will take us.

Notes

1 As the author has argued elsewhere (Francis Seton, 'The Question of Ideological Obstacles to Rational Price Setting in Communist Countries', in Alan Abouchar (ed.), *The Socialist Price Mechanism*, Duke University Press, Durham, NC, 1977, pp. 10–39), this furnishes what may be termed the Marxian definition of labour-value 'by imputation', which is paralleled by and in certain circumstances equivalent to a second Marxian definition of the same measure, the definition 'by alienation', derived by positing a uniform 'rate of exploitation' (surplus-to-wages ratio) in all lines of production.

2 The essential Marxian qualification that the labour in question must be 'socially necessary', which opens up a number of bolt-holes to defenders who would bring down this definition from the height of unreason, is here omitted as irrelevant to our particular purpose.

3 So far we have distinguished or implied seven of these:

$$\left.\begin{array}{ll}\text{coal lira} & \text{clr}\\ \text{power-lira} & \text{plr}\\ \text{service-lira} & \text{slr}\end{array}\right\}\text{glr}\qquad\qquad \left.\begin{array}{ll}\text{capital-lira} & \text{clr}\\ \text{labour-lira} & \text{llr}\\ \text{money-unit} & \$\end{array}\right\}\text{flr}$$

plus the 'perun' (˙/.), which will be used to qualify pure, dimensionless numbers or ratios by analogy with percentages (28% = 0.28˙/.) wherever the usual notation (0.28) is not explicit enough.

4
'USE FETISHISM'

4a Commodity-norming

The valuation of commodities according to their *costs*, i.e. their absorption of input-commodities and factors that can be 'debited' to them, is so ingrained in our intuition through age-old habit and convention that it takes a major conceptual effort to grasp and countenance the valuation by the 'opposite' principle, that of *use* or utility. In the Marxian system, for instance, the 'value-in-use' of a commodity makes its appearance as hardly more than an *obiter dictum*, a mere supplement to the cost-based 'value-in-exchange' which is defined as the full labour-cost discussed in the last chapter. It is only the latter that is invested with an 'objective' social existence independent of human subjectivity and individual whim. The former features merely as a *precondition* for the existence of value, and not as a measure of it.[1]

As an 'experiment in thought', however, there is no logical reason why we should not adopt the alternative method of valuation dependent on the *uses* that a commodity serves, and 'credit' it with its contribution to these uses rather than debiting it with the contribution of the resources that it absorbs.

Let us start with a 'monomaniac' scheme in which only *one* final good, say coal, is held to be of benefit to final users, and all other products and factors are valued only to the extent that they serve the production of coal (just as, under 'labour-cost monomania', only the absorption of labour was accounted a cost to the economy, all other inputs being valued only to the extent that they themselves absorbed labour). In such a scheme a unit (lr) of any commodity would receive a 'credit' – to be termed a 'norm' – which would depend on whether it was used in coal production, power generation, or the provision of services (as in Table 3.1), since all these branches served to safeguard the final uses of coal, either directly or indirectly, as providers of inputs to the coal industry; it would receive no credit for the final services it rendered directly, since these were irrelevant to the coal industry. Only coal itself would receive a 'credit' (clr/lr) for its final-use contribution to GNP.

A 'credit' of this sort can be described as a 'price' only by remote analogy – by virtue of the fact that it is a 'tag' or 'label' pinned on units of a commodity. It does not – as normal prices do – attach to the commodity *per se* (as defined by its sector of *origin* in our scheme), but only to its *use* (defined by its sector of *destination*), thus valuing the same unit differentially according to its function in the economy, regardless of its intrinsic characteristics or gestation. Since 'price' or 'cost' would seem to be misleading appellations for this form of assessment, we propose the use of the term 'norm', and will speak of 'coal-norms', 'power-norms', or 'service-norms', depending on which of these sectors is selected for the role of ultimate (exclusive) standard of use-valuations.

What, then, are the correct 'coal-norms' in the economy of the scheme in Table 3.2? They must be a set of coefficients of dimension clr/lr which, when used to norm the three uses distinguished by the columns of this scheme, will sum to the valuation of the corresponding outputs normed in the same way. We can show that they are equal to 0.45, 0.14, and 0 clr/lr by the row-wise additions of Table 4.1. This scheme ensures that the direct (final-use) and indirect norm-contributions add up exactly to the correspondingly normed outputs, with the 'standard good', coal, making the only positively normed direct contribution and all others receiving zero norms for their final uses, in line with our 'coal-monomaniac' assessment. Since any triad of norms deviating from (0.45, 0.14, 0) would destroy these identities, we can assert that these three figures (expressed in clr/lr) are indeed the correct 'coal-norms' of our three commodities.

In a similar way we can show that the three norms based on *power* rather than coal as the standard of norming will be 0.05, 0.32, and

Table 4.1

Cdty. inputs	Coal ind.		Power ind.		Service ind.	Indirect use norms		Direct use norms		Full use norms
Coal	36 clr	+	1.5 clr	+	0 clr	37.5	+	30	=	67.5 clr
Power	9 clr	+	3.5 clr	+	0 clr	12.5	+	0	=	12.5 clr
Services	0 clr	+	0 clr	+	0 clr	0	+	0	=	0 clr

Table 4.2

Cdty. inputs	Coal ind.	Power ind.	Services ind.	Indirect use-norm		Direct use-norm		Full use-norm
Coal	4 plr	3.5 plr	0 plr	7.5	+	0	=	7.5 plr
Power	1 plr	8 plr	0 plr	9	+	20	=	29 plr
Services	0 plr	0 plr	0 plr	0	+	0	=	0 plr

0 plr/lr, since their use would yield the scheme (rounded to the nearest $\frac{1}{2}$ plr) of Table 4.2. This time, of course, it is the final uses of *power* that are the only ones allowed a positive use-norm (1 plr/lr).

Lastly, we can show that the adoption of *services* as the norm-standard would entail commodity-norms equal to 0.51, 0.54, and 1 slr/lr, thus yielding the scheme (in rounded figures) of Table 4.3.

Table 4.3

Cdty. inputs	Coal ind.		Power ind.		Services ind.	Indirect use-norm		Direct use-norm		Full use-norm
Coal	41 slr	+	5.5 slr	+	30 slr	76.5	+	0	=	76.5
Power	10 slr	+	13.5 slr	+	25 slr	48.5	+	0	=	48.5
Services	0 slr	+	0 slr	+	10 slr	10	+	75	=	85

To sum up, our 'monomaniac' norming on the basis of coal, power, and services as the standard commodities respectively entails the commodity-norms appearing in the columns of the matrix:

$$\begin{pmatrix} 0.45 & 0.05 & 0.51 \\ 0.14 & 0.32 & 0.54 \\ 0.00 & 0.00 & 1.00 \end{pmatrix} \tag{4.1}$$

4b Factor-norming

The norming of factor-inputs according to their uses by means of the commodity-norms above yields the norm to be attributed to each of the factors per unit of its use. Thus, if coal-norms are opted for, the calculations yield 0.17 and 0.26 clr as the norms of a factor-lira of capital and labour respectively, since – referring to Table 3.2 and matrix (4.1) – we have:

$$\begin{aligned} 6 \times 0.45 + 18 \times 0.14 + 6 \times 0 &= 30 \times 0.17 \\ 39 \times 0.45 + 27 \times 0.14 + 17 \times 0 &= 83 \times 0.26. \end{aligned} \tag{4.2}$$

Similar procedures yield the power- and service-based norms of the two factors in terms of plr and slr. A conspectus of the two factor-norms based on the three alternative commodities as standards for norming is given by the matrix:

$$\begin{pmatrix} 0.17 & 0.26 \\ 0.20 & 0.13 \\ 0.63 & 0.62 \end{pmatrix} \tag{4.3}$$

The reader can easily test the second and third rows of the matrix by analogy with (4.2) above.

We are thus presented with three alternative ways of factor-norming, but are given no clue as to which of them, or what combination of them, would furnish the single most rational pair of factor-norms. A basis for such rationality could be provided only if the commodities were allocated relative weights, say p_1, p_2, and p_3, which would then be transferred to the factor-norms of matrix (4.3), resulting in the composite norms:

$$\begin{matrix} 0.17p_1 + 0.20p_2 + 0.63p_3 \\ 0.26p_1 + 0.13p_2 + 0.62p_3 \end{matrix} \tag{4.4}$$

for capital and labour, respectively. In conventional terms, these figures are probably best described as the average (and marginal) 'revenue productivities' of the two factors when commodity prices are fixed at p_1, p_2, and p_3.

In a later chapter we shall give algebraic derivations for the commodity- and factor-norms illustrated above, and show justification for the interpretation offered in the preceding paragraph.

Note

1 Karl Marx, *Capital*, Part 1, Chapter 1, Section 1, Moore-Aveling translation of 3rd German edn., W. Glaisher Ltd, London, 1920, pp. 5–8.

5

EIGENPRICES

So far, our ability to determine single cost-prices for goods or use-prices (norms) for factors has been dependent on the arbitrary initial assumption of a price-set for the opposite pole of the economic circuit, i.e. for factors as they transform themselves into goods, or for goods as they generate demand for factors. We must now enquire whether this remaining indeterminacy in the pricing process can be overcome, and cast about for criteria to determine the initial choice.

To start with, we shall test the arbitrary assumption that a lira-worth of labour is 'worth' twice as much as a lira-worth of capital, thus setting the initial factor-norms f_1, f_2 of Section 3a equal to 1 and 2 respectively, and the mark-up for full-costing at 27 per cent. In line with (3.2), this would imply full costs of 2, 1.7, and 2 for the three commodities respectively, as may be seen from Table 5.1. If these values are now accepted, they would, by virtue of expression (4.4), imply factor-norms of 1.94 and 1.98 for capital and labour. By this token, therefore, our original assumption 'overvalued' labour by some 2 per cent and 'undervalued' capital by approximately 94 per cent. If we had started from the arbitrary assumptions of commodity-values equal to the previously computed full costs (i.e., 2, 1.7, and 2), which, as we have seen, would have implied factor norms of 1.94 and 1.98, the revised full costs of commodities (including a 27 per cent mark-up) would have been 2.18, 2.05, and 2.33 (by virtue of (3.2)). In this case, therefore, our initial assumption would have 'undervalued' the commodities by approximately 18, 8, and 33 per cent respectively. If we tried to reproduce the original estimate for coal by reducing the mark-up from 27 to 17 per cent, we would be left with an initial 'undervaluation' of power by some 10 per cent and of services by over 14 per cent, and it is clear that no tampering with the mark-up could reproduce the initial estimates for all three commodities at once.

The initial assumptions we have made thus imply price systems that reward some or all factor-owners for contributions that they are not making to the final users of commodities, or compensate some or all producers (factor-users) in excess of the full costs (including 'normal profits') that they have incurred. Other arbitrary initial assumptions could have resulted in rewards or penalties for factor-owners and/or producers that lacked economic justification in a similar way, or possibly in a mixture of unjustified rewards and penalties. No price system of this kind can be accepted as fully self-consistent or 'rational'.

To find a system free from these defects, we must cast about for an initial estimate for factor-norms which, after appropriate allowance for mark-up, will *generate commodity-costs that imply the same factor-norms from which we started.* We can show that the only norm and mark-up set fulfilling this condition is the set 1, 1, and 11 per cent. If capital and labour received equal norms of unity and the 'normal profit' is set at 11 per cent, the full costs of the three commodities will be 0.97, 0.91, and 1.03 respectively. Conversely, if the latter figures are accepted as the 'proper' prices of the commodities, the factor-norms turn out to be 1, 1 again, as they were originally estimated to be. The full set of prices for goods and factors (0.97, 0.91, 1.03, 1, 1) thus forms a self-consistent set (given the uniform mark-up rate of 11 per cent), in the sense that all commodities are 'priced at full cost' and all factors 'costed at full price', and none of the values contain elements that cannot be economically justified. As we shall see in a later chapter, this price system is unique up to a multiplicative constant, given the input–output scheme assumed, and may be regarded as 'proper' to it. It will be termed the 'eigenprice' system of the economy in question. Any deviation from it in the price system in actual operation should be taken as prima facie evidence of irrationality, the existence of price elements that may be justified on historical, social, or moral grounds, but cannot claim a purely economic base. The explanatory chapter will also offer an economic interpretation of the mark-up associated with the eigenprice system, a special form of social surplus, to be known as the economy's 'eigenyield'.

Table 5.1 summarizes the three experiments undertaken in the test above, to show that arbitrary choices of norms, commodity prices and mark-ups will in general result in inconsistent (or 'irrational') price systems, while only one particular set, associated with a proper mark-up, will result in a consistent structure – the economy's 'eigenprices'.

Table 5.1

	Factor-norms f_1	f_2	Mark-up σ	Cost ratio $\phi = \frac{1}{1+\sigma}$	Goods prices p_1	p_2	p_3
Posited	1	2	0.27	0.79			
Implied*					2	1.7	2
Posited					2	1.7	2
Implied†	1.94	1.98					
Posited	1.94	1.98					
Implied*					2.17	2.05	2.34
Posited					2	1.7	2
Implied†	1.94	1.98					
Posited	1.94	1.98	0.17	0.85			
Implied*					2	1.90	2.15
Posited	1	1	0.11	0.90			
Implied*					0.97	0.91	1.03
Posited					0.97	0.91	1.03
Implied†	1	1					

*As per (3.2); i.e.,

$$p_1 = \frac{0.17f_1 + 0.70f_2}{\phi}, p_2 = \frac{0.30f_1 + 0.52f_2}{\phi}, p_3 = \frac{0.25f_1 + 0.68f_2}{\phi}.$$

†As per (4.4); i.e.,

$$f_1 = 0.17p_1 + 0.20p_2 + 0.63p_3, f_2 = 0.26p_1 + 0.13p_2 + 0.62p_3.$$

6
THE BASIC SCHEME IN ALGEBRAIC TERMS

For a rigorous definition of the concepts introduced in the last three chapters we must systematize our *tableau economique* and replace the randomly chosen arithmetic by generalized schemata of an algebraic nature. We do so in (6.1) below, which illustrates an economy of $n\,(=3)$ production sectors using $m\,(=2)$ non-produced inputs of 'factors' (say, capital and labour) in the shape of an input–output table of three quadrants. In the second (north-east) quadrant we distinguish $k(=4)$ final uses, say, net exports, government, household consumption, and fixed investment, together making up each sector's total 'yield' (y) which, when added to its re-processed output or 'throughput' (row-sum of x), make up the total output of the sector (z). Both factor-inputs and end-uses are identified by superscripts, as are the destinations of sectoral inputs, whose sector origins are shown as subscripts; i.e., x^j_i stands for sector i's deliveries to sector j, y^s_i sector i's deliveries to end-use s, and w^j_r factor r's absorption in the product of sector j.[1] The last row of τ stands for residual surpluses and taxes entering into the formation of prices.

$$
\begin{aligned}
&x_1^1 + x_1^2 + x_1^3 + y_1^1 + y_1^2 + y_1^3 + y_1^4 &&= z_1 \\
&x_2^1 + x_2^2 + x_2^3 + y_2^1 + y_2^2 + y_2^3 + y_2^4 &&= z_2 \\
&x_3^1 + x_3^2 + x_3^3 + y_3^1 + y_3^2 + y_3^3 + y_3^4 &&= z_3 \\
&w_1^1 + w_1^2 + w_1^3 &&= w_1 \\
&w_2^1 + w_2^2 + w_2^3 &&= w_2 \\
&\tau^1 + \tau^2 + \tau^3 &&= \tau
\end{aligned}
\qquad (6.1)
$$

All flows are assumed to be homogeneous,[2] each valued uniformly at a single price as actually traded during a given year at user prices (i.e. inclusive of all taxes),[3] so that the sum of any column equals the sum of the corresponding row; i.e.,

$$(\acute{\xi} + \acute{\omega} + \acute{\tau})' = \grave{x} + \grave{y} = \grave{z} \tag{6.2}$$

from which the traditional national income identity may be derived by simple summation;[4] i.e.,

$$\acute{\omega}\grave{\imath} + \tau = \acute{\imath}\grave{y} = y_0 \tag{6.3}$$

Putting tableau (6.1) in matrix form (and generalizing the number of sectors, factors, and end-uses to n, m, and k respectively), we can write

$$\begin{aligned} X\grave{\imath} + \grave{y} &= \grave{z} \\ W\grave{\imath} &= \grave{w} \end{aligned} \tag{6.4}$$

where it is understood that each output z_i will depend on the productive inputs listed in the ith columns of matrices X and W. Given that this dependence is of the usual proportional and 'limitational' kind, involving fixed input-coefficients, we can write this as

$$\begin{aligned} A\grave{z} + \grave{y} &= \grave{z} \\ B\grave{z} &= \grave{w} \end{aligned} \tag{6.5}$$

where the new symbols stand for the 'coefficient matrices' (of material and primary inputs respectively):

$$A = X\hat{z}^{-1} \text{ and } B = W\hat{z}^{-1}. \tag{6.6}$$

The upper portion of (6.5) is clearly equivalent to $\grave{y} = (I - A)\grave{z}$ and therefore yields the familiar formula for the output targets needed to create a prescribed 'final bill of goods' $\grave{y}$:[5]

$$\grave{z} = (I - A)^{-1}\grave{y} \equiv \bar{A}^{\urcorner}\grave{y}. \tag{6.7}$$

It should be stressed at this point that, while we do not deny the dependence of A and B on prevailing prices or other variables with feedback effects, it will be our assumption throughout this book that the coefficients observed in a given year have already undergone a process of optimal adaptation to underlying preferences, aspirations, and constraints, whether perceived by atomistic producers in the light of market signals or directly selected by planners, policy-makers, or dictators. We shall therefore accept them as given and focus attention on the *ex post* evaluation of the static structure that is found to have resulted.

Notes

1 As exercises of this kind are apt to result in a confusing proliferation of notational devices, a systematic directory of the most frequently occurring symbols for the convenience of readers appears as Appendix A of this book. For the rest, we hope to add to notational clarity by using acute and grave accents (´, `) over corresponding letters for row- and column-vectors respectively, a circumflex (ˆ) for diagonal matrices, unaccented capital letters for other matrices, and unaccented lower-case letters for scalars. In particular I will stand for the unit matrix, $\acute{\imath}_r$, $\grave{\imath}^r$ for its rth row and column vectors, and $\acute{\imath}$, $\grave{\imath}$ for the all-unit vectors (with 1 in all positions). In stating origins and destinations of flows we replace the usual double-subscript notation by the subscription–superscript convention, which will enable us to write the constituent columns and rows of matrices unambiguously by quoting only the relevant affix in the proper position, e.g. the jth column of matrix X, as $\grave{x}^j$, and its ith row as $\acute{x}_i$; the sectoral inputs of the rth factor are thus $\acute{w}_r$ and the components of the sth end-use, $\grave{y}^s$. In addition, the total row and column sums will be denoted by the corresponding *lower-case* Roman and Greek letters, respectively:

$$X\grave{\imath} = \grave{x} \qquad \acute{\imath}X = \acute{\xi}$$

$$Y\grave{\imath} = \grave{y} \qquad \acute{\imath}Y = \acute{\eta}$$

$$W\grave{\imath} = \grave{w} \qquad \acute{\imath}W = \acute{\omega} \quad \text{etc.}$$

We retain the conventional use of the prime sign (′) to denote transposition of rows into columns or vice versa.

2 It should be noted that our model does not allow for joint production of any sort, although the extensions necessary for this would no doubt be possible.

3 In principle, each row should be measured in terms of its own physical units, but we prefer to use surrogates for this in terms of a single notional currency, the ‘lira’, which enables different rows to be added together when this is required for accounting purposes, or to be dimensionally differentiated by distinguishing ‘factor-liras’ (flr) from ‘goods-liras’ (glr) or single-commodity liras (coal liras, power liras, etc.) when this is indicated in the interests of dimensional clarity.

4 For the sake of simplicity, we dispense with a fourth (south-east) quadrant for factor-inputs going directly to final uses (e.g. teaching, medical treatment, administration, etc.), by assuming that such inputs are routed through a special sector subsumed under service industries and relayed to final users as part of a sectoral contribution,

say y_3^2. This enables us to represent the GNP as the simple sum of the y in the second quadrant, which can all be revalued in line with ordinary sectoral commodities.

5 For conceptual conciseness and to save space, we introduce the inverted L as a superscript to denote the 'Leontif inverse' of a matrix; i.e.,

$$A^{\urcorner} \equiv (I - A)^{-1}, \; Q^{\urcorner} \equiv (I - Q)^{-1}, \text{ etc.}$$

which could be read, say, 'A lin', 'Q lin', etc.

7
THE 'FULL-COST PRICING' OF COMMODITIES – VALUATION BY COST

Suppose now that a 'cost-monomaniac' value theory adopts the rth factor in (6.1) as the single 'cost-standard' whose total (direct and indirect) absorption per unit of each product furnishes the products' cost-values $\acute{c}_r = (c_r^1, c_r^2, \ldots, c_r^n)$.[1] For any product i these values must obviously satisfy the equation:

$$c_r^i = b_r^i + (a_1^i c_r^1 + a_2^i c_r^2, \ldots, + a_n^i c_r^n) = b_r^i + \acute{c}_r \grave{a}^i \qquad (7.1)$$

which defines cost-value on the given basis r as the sum of direct and indirect (in brackets) absorption of factor r per unit output of the product under valuation. Since this is true for all n products, it can be written in matrix form:

$$\acute{c}_r = \acute{b}_r + \acute{c}_r A \qquad (7.2)$$

or explicitly as

$$\acute{c}_r = \acute{b}_r \overline{A}\rceil. \qquad (7.3)$$

If r stands for the factor 'homogeneous labour', the c_r are evidently the Marxian labour-values as defined by the imputation of all commodity-values to the single factor labour, with other factors arbitrarily excluded from any part in the formation of true value and their incomes ascribed merely to socially sanctioned exploitation.

It will be noted that the Leontief inverse $\overline{A}\rceil$ acts here as a 'synthesizer' in converting the *direct* labour costs $\acute{b}_r$ into *full* (direct and indirect) labour costs through simple post-multiplication. The latter are therefore seen to be quantifiable, subject only to acceptance of our 'lira'-yardstick as the correct measure of homogeneous labour, and their numerical values can be obtained by a familiar computer process, given a knowledge of A and $\acute{b}_r$.

Formally, of course, we can cast any of the $m-1$ factors other than labour in the role of 'cost-basis', thus obtaining as many alternative sets of single-factor cost-values for our n products as there are factors. A conspectus of these would take the form of the 'cost-matrix'

$$C = B\overline{A}^{\rceil} \tag{7.4}$$

where each set is displayed in a row of n values, with each of the m factors in turn doing duty as the 'cost-basis' as we move from row to row, and the typical element c_r^i denoting the cost of product i in terms of factor r. The first row might give the 'capital-values', the second the 'labour-values', the third the 'land-' or 'import'-values, etc. But ideology or doctrine apart, we have no criterion for accepting any of these as economically or logically superior to the others. If dyed-in-the-wool capitalists had any stomach for writing economics, they might well put forward a 'capital theory of value'. No doubt, as Tugan-Baranovsky once said, if horses could write economics, we might be taught a 'horsepower theory of value'.[2] But short of such one-sided verdicts, we could arrive at single, unambiguous cost-values for our set of commodities only if we had prior valuations (norms) for the primary factors, say $\acute{f} = (f_1, f_2, \ldots, f_m)$, which would allow us to let each of them enter into the formation of commodity-values with a pre-assigned relative weight. The composite cost-value of commodity i, say $c^i(f)$, would then emerge as

$$f_1 c_1^i + f_2 c_2^i \ldots + f_m c_m^i$$

or in matrix form:

$$\acute{c}(f) = \acute{f} C. \tag{7.5}$$

To complete our full-cost pricing, however, we must allow for a uniform mark-up, say, $100\,(1-\phi)/\phi$ per cent to add the usual surplus (profit or tax) to factor-costs (7.5), thus yielding

$$\acute{p}(f) = \frac{1}{\phi}\acute{f} C \tag{7.6}$$

for the 'composite full costs' of commodities. The introduction of the profit rate $\sigma(=(1-\phi)/\phi)$ presents us with one degree of freedom in addition to f, which will stand us in good stead in later stages of the analysis.

So far, however, we have no rational basis for choosing any set of prior factor-norms $\acute{f}$ in preference to any other; and unless ideology, received doctrine, or some form of social ethics can lead us to such an *a priori* choice, we must continue our quest.

Notes

1 The products being valued are identified by the superscripts of c and the bases of valuation by the subscripts; thus c_r^j stands for the cost-value of commodity j on the cost-basis (of factor) r.
2 We owe this quote to Professor A. Nove of Glasgow.

8

THE 'FULL-PRICE COSTING' OF FACTORS – VALUATION BY USE

All value-measures reviewed in the last chapter were aggregations of cost elements derived from the side of factor supply, without regard to the utilities of products as determined by the demand for final goods. In the interests of a genuinely comprehensive and unified concept of value,[1] we must now abandon this type of 'cost-fetishism' and turn – as a first step – to the opposite extreme, a one-sided view of value informed by utilities only and fully deserving the opprobrium of 'use-fetishism'.

As in the case of cost-fetishism, we shall start with the extreme, 'monomaniac', form of the disease, and assume that the final use of only *one* commodity, say y_k, is adjudged to be of true benefit to the economy, and that all other commodities and uses are credited with usefulness only to the extent that they contribute to the satisfaction of the selected use, whether directly, through the production of commodity k, or indirectly, by serving that production as an input. We are thus defining the 'k-based norms' $(v_k^1, v_k^2, \ldots, v_k^n)$ as follows:

$$z_i v_k^i = y_j + (x_i^1 v_k^1 + x_i^2 v_k^2 \ldots + x_i^n v_k^n) \tag{8.1}$$

giving expression to the fact that the total 'norm-credit' awarded to the production of sector i must be equal to its *direct* credit for contributing to final uses of $k(y_j = y_k$ if $j = k$, otherwise $= 0)$ and to the *indirect* credit earned by providing inputs to other sectors to the extent they themselves contribute to y_k (the bracketed expression). Dividing both sides of (8.1) by z_i, we obtain the fully explicit definition

$$v_k^i = m_k + (q_i^1 v_k^1 + q_i^2 v_k^2, \ldots, q_i^n v_k^n) \tag{8.2}$$

where q are the output quotas of sector i allocated to the various i-consuming sectors of the economy $(q_i^r \equiv x_i^r / z_i)$, not to be confused with the input-coefficients $a_i^r (\equiv x_i^r / z_r)$ used in cost analysis earlier, the matrices A and Q being defined as

$$A = Xz^{-1} \text{ and } Q = \hat{z}^{-1} X \tag{8.3}$$

respectively. The symbol m_k stands for the 'final-use quota' y_k / z_k, thus implying $\hat{m} \equiv \hat{z}^{-1} \hat{y}$.

The definition (8.2) can be put more conveniently in matrix form:

$$\grave{v}_k = \hat{m} \grave{\imath}_k + Q \grave{v}_k \tag{8.4}$$

where $\grave{\imath}_k$ stands for the kth column of the unit matrix, containing 1 in the kth place and zero everywhere else. Clearly, (8.4) implies $(I - Q) \grave{v}_k = \hat{m} \grave{\imath}_k$, and therefore the fully explicit matrix definition:

$$\grave{v}_k = \overline{Q}^{\rceil} \hat{m} \grave{\imath}_k . \tag{8.5}$$

To obviate the arbitrary choice of a commodity to serve as the 'use-base' k, we could allow every commodity a contribution to the final uses of the economy with a (so far arbitrary) weight p, thus replacing $\grave{\imath}_k$ in (8.5) by a list of commodity-prices $\grave{p}$, and obtain the general composite-norm equation:

$$\grave{v}(\acute{p}) = \overline{Q}^{\rceil} \hat{m} \grave{p} . \tag{8.6}$$

This is the analog of the explicit full-cost equation (7.5), with the important difference that commodity-valuations are now derived by aggregating contributions to final yields $(\grave{y})$ instead of summing calls on primary resources $(\acute{w})$.

From here it is only a short step to the use-valuation ('norming') of factors $(\grave{n})$ by the summation of their contributions to the several commodities they help to produce; i.e.,

$$\hat{w} \grave{n} = W \grave{v} \tag{8.7}$$

or, after pre-division by $\hat{w}$, and defining the 'factor-quota' matrix $R \equiv \hat{w}^{-1} W$,

$$\grave{n} = R \grave{v} = R \overline{Q}^{\rceil} \hat{m} \grave{p} . \tag{8.8}$$

Finally, transposing (8.8) for analogy with (7.5) and (7.6), we obtain

$$\acute{n}(p) = \acute{p} \hat{m} \overline{Q}^{\rceil\prime} R' \equiv \acute{p} N \tag{8.9}$$

where N is the 'norm-matrix' $\hat{m} \overline{Q}^{\rceil\prime} R'$. As in the case of the cost matrix C, the meaning of the norm-matrix[2] N can be made clear by setting $\acute{p}$ equal to a row of the unit-matrix, say $\acute{\imath}_k$, which assumes that only the kth final yield y_k is credited with utility (measured in its own terms) while all others are deemed to make zero contributions to the final benefit accruing to the economy. This shows that the kth row of N records the norms of the m primary inputs in terms of their contribution to the single yield y_k. Just as C was shown to be a conspectus of 'single-factor product costs', so N is now shown to be a conspectus of 'single-yield factor-norms'. The traditional 'cost-monomania' of *single-factor* theories of value has been stood on its head to turn into the 'use-monomania' of *single-yield* theory, and if this is generalized by admitting ***all*** factors and yields to value formation through pre-assigned relative weights $\acute{f}$ and $\acute{p}$, we generate 'shadow-prices' for products and factors as shown by the mappings or 'transformations' (7.6) and (8.9); i.e.

$$\acute{p}(f) = \frac{1}{\phi_*} \acute{f}C \text{ and } \acute{n}(p) = \acute{p}N \qquad (8.10)$$

which will be termed the 'downstream' and 'upstream' transformations, respectively. The asterisk added to ϕ in (8.10) is of no significance here, but anticipates the notation introduced in Chapter 12.

Notes

1 Advocates of exclusively cost-based valuations such as Marx were of course perfectly aware that their 'value-in-exchange' did not account for all the attributes attaching to the normal concept of value, and posited the existence of 'value-in-use' as a parallel and complementary category. They did not, however, follow mainstream economists in their attempts to integrate both aspects of value in a single concept, and resigned themselves to living with a somewhat uncomfortable dichotomy.

2 The idea of input–output analysis based on 'quotas' as well as 'input-coefficients' and certain considerations deriving from it is not without antecedents. (See e.g. Maria Augustinovics, 'Methods of International and Intertemporal Comparison of Structure', Chapter 13 in A.P. Carter and A. Bródy (eds), *Contributions to Input–Output Analysis*, North-Holland Publishing Company, Amsterdam/London, 1970.) The purpose of that exercise, however, is the quest for an aspect of economic structure invariant to the price system rather than the search for a system of universal pricing or valuation as such.

9
ALTERNATIVE INTERPRETATIONS OF 'USE-NORMS'

9a 'Yield-productivity'

So far we have derived the factor-norms by a process of conceptual inversion, whereby a single selected commodity had its final supply ('yield') cast in the role of ultimate determinant of value, to be traced 'upstream' to the other end of the economy for analysis into derivative use-values ('norms') attaching to the factors engaged in its production – just as, in more familiar types of analyses, the contributions of a single factor (e.g. labour) are traced 'downstream', to be integrated into the cost-values of the end-products that they help to create. To alleviate the strain that such an inversion must exert on our faculties of conceptualization, we offer a more direct interpretation, which can be made to follow immediately from the definitional equation (8.9) if we remind ourselves that the definitions of A as $X\hat{z}^{-1}$ and Q as $\hat{z}^{-1}X$ (8.3) imply the relationships

$$Q = \hat{z}^{-1}A\hat{z} \text{ and } \overline{Q}\rceil = \hat{z}^{-1}\overline{A}\rceil\hat{z} \tag{9.1}$$

while those of R as $\hat{w}^{-1}W$ and B as $W\hat{z}^{-1}$ ((8.7) and (6.6)) imply

$$R = \hat{w}^{-1}B\hat{z}. \tag{9.2}$$

Accordingly, the norm-matrix N, defined in (8.9), may be explained as

$$N = \hat{m}\overline{Q}\rceil'R' = (\hat{y}\hat{z}^{-1})(\hat{z}\overline{A}\rceil'\hat{z}^{-1})(\hat{z}B'\hat{w}^{-1}) = \hat{y}\overline{A}\rceil'B'\hat{w}^{-1}$$

which by virtue of (6.4) simplifies to

$$N = \hat{y}C'\hat{w}^{-1}. \tag{9.3}$$

On the right-hand side of this equation the full-cost matrix C' is pre-multiplied by the diagonal matrix of yields ($\hat{y}$), thus resulting in a conspectus of final yields valued at the full single-factor cost based on each factor in turn ($\hat{y}C'$). i.e. a conspectus of what might be called the 'yield-products' of the factors. When this is post-divided by the total factor-uses ($\hat{w}$), it will result in the 'sectoral yield-productivities' of the factors at full-cost valuation.

We have thus analysed the total contribution of a unit of each factor evaluated in its own terms into such portions as may be 'debited' to each of the sectors according to the yield generated by the direct and indirect use which that sector makes of the factors concerned.[1] The factor-norms simply measure the total credit accruing to each factor per unit when its sector credits are valued in the commodity-price system $\acute{p}$, i.e. $\acute{p}N$, and are therefore unique projections or 'mappings' of the product prices assumed.

9b The generation of factor norms – 'norming' circulation

Our inbred conceptions and traditions have made us conscious that in practice full commodity-costs are generated by a mandatory flow of money-tokens which requires every sector to 'pay' for its inputs and to replace these payments fully by claiming in turn compensation for them at the uniform rate of its own costs for every unit product delivered to its clients. In this way the prices of the factors of production are 'passed on' to the final users of commodities who are ultimately responsible for their total discharge.

A similar money circulation under an imaginary, though fully practicable, régime would generate our factor-norms from a given set of commodity-prices. Let us consider this 'norm-generating' circulation in the simplest case of 'use-monomania', where only one commodity, say good 1 (coal), ranks for final benefit; i.e., the point of departure is a commodity-price structure of (1, 0, 0), taking our cue from the arithmetic exercise of Chapter 4. The government or planning commission would then start by issuing to the coal industry (or bank) y_1 units of its special currency, i.e. 30 clr (if we are guided by Chapter 4's example). The coal bank would ascertain that it had been awarded 30 clr for an output of 150 lr, i.e. an 'initial norm' of 0.20 clr/lr. It would then be required to unload this issue by paying into the banks of its supplying sectors and factor-inputs ('capital bank' and 'labour bank') a 'first-round' distribution equal to their respective deliveries to the coal industry multiplied by that initial norm, leaving any residual profit or tax to be paid at the same rate (in this case, 5 lr at 0.20 clr/lr, i.e. 1 clr) into a special 'tax bank' *T*. Alternatively, we may say that the initial issue of 30 clr must be completely unloaded to its input-providers (including the tax bank) in strict proportion to their deliveries to the coal industry. After the 'first-round' distribution, every sector and every factor providing inputs to the coal industry would find a 'first-round' clr deposit in its bank from which it could compute its 'first-round norm'; e.g., 16/150 = 0.11 clr/lr for the coal industry, 4/90 = 0.04 clr/lr for the power industry, 1/12 = 0.08 clr/lr for the tax banks, etc. It would now have to act exactly as the coal bank had done after the initial issue, i.e. unload the total of its clr deposit in a 'second-round' distribution to the banks of its own input-providers (including the tax bank) at the rate of its own 'first-round' norm per unit delivery, i.e. in strict proportion to their deliveries to itself. It is as though each sector owed its suppliers and production factors (including itself as residual earner) a 'dividend' in proportion not to capital invested, but to input-value contributed, where the total subject to distribution was not the net profit, but the gross dividend income received by the sector itself. The sector and factor banks (as well as the tax bank) would thus find a 'reflux' of clr from their first-round payments in the shape of second-round deposits returned to them by some or all of the sectors they had just paid. Only the factor and tax banks would be exempt from such refluxes as they are by definition free from 'suppliers' to whom the clr-deposits would have to be unloaded, and can simply allow successive clr deposits to accumulate in their vaults. The sector banks, however, would be obliged to *distribute* the sum of the successive clr receipts of each round (always at the rate of their own latest 'norm' per unit delivery), and to do likewise with the sum of the resulting 'refluxes' at the next round, until these refluxes had shrunk to negligible proportions. When this has happened, they will each be left without significant clr deposits and the whole of the initial issue of 30 clr will have found its way into the factor and tax banks. In each of these banks the cumulative total received divided by the total supply of the relevant factor will then equal the factor-norms as we have defined them.

Clearly, the power- or service-based factor-norms could be generated in the same way as the coal-norms, by simply changing the initial issue from one of y_1 clr to the coal industry to one of y_2 plr to the power industry or one of y_3 slr to the service industry. The composite factor-norms based on arbitrary commodity-prices of p_1, p_2, and p_3 would require an initial issue of $p_1 y_1$ lr to the coal industry and $p_2 y_2$

Table 9.1 *The generation of norms* (minor discrepancies due to rounding)

'Round'	Input	X			z	Distr.* δ	Incr.** γ δ/z	Cum⁺ γ
	C	80	10	30	150	30	0.20	0.20
	P	20	25	25	90	0	0	0
	S	0	0	10	85	0	0	0
(0)	K	6	18	6	30	0	0	0
	L	39	27	17	83	0	0	0
	T	150	10	−3	12	0	0	0
	Sum	150	90	85	–	–	–	–
	C	16	0	0	150	16	0.11	0.31
	P	4	0	0	90	4	0.04	0.04
	S	0	0	0	85	0	0	0
(1)	K	1.2	0	0	30	1.2	0.04	0.04
	L	7.8	0	0	83	7.8	0.09	0.09
	T	1	0	0	12	1	0.08	0.08
	Sum	30	0	0	–	–	–	–
	C	8.54	0.44	0	150	8.97	0.06	0.37
	P	2.13	1.11	0	90	3.24	0.04	0.08
	S	0	0	0	85	0	0	0
(2)	K	0.64	0.80	0	30	1.44	0.05	0.09
	L	4.16	1.21	0	83	5.36	0.06	0.16
	T	0.53	0.44	0	12	0.97	0.08	0.16
	Sum	0.16	4	0	–	–	–	–
	C	4.78	0.36	0	150	5.14	0.03	0.40
	P	1.20	0.90	0	90	2.10	0.02	0.10
	S	0	0	0	85	0	0	0
(3)	K	0.36	0.65	0	30	1.01	0.03	0.12
	L	2.33	0.97	0	83	3.30	0.04	0.20
	T	0.30	0.36	0	12	0.66	0.05	0.22
	Sum	8.97	3.24	0	–	–	–	–
	C	2.74	0.23	0	150	2.98	0.02	0.42
	P	0.69	0.58	0	90	1.27	0.01	0.11
	S	0	0	0	85	0	0	0
(4)	K	0.21	0.42	0	30	0.62	0.02	0.14
	L	1.34	0.63	0	83	2.00	0.02	0.22
	T	0.17	0.23	0	12	0.40	0.03	0.25
	Sum	5.14	2.10	0	–	–	–	–
	C	1.59	0.14	0	150	1.73	0.01	0.43
	P	0.40	0.35	0	90	0.75	0.01	0.12
	S	0	0	0	85	0	0	0
(5)	K	0.12	0.25	0	30	0.37	0.01	0.15
	L	0.77	0.38	0	83	0.15	0.01	0.24
	T	0.10	0.14	0	12	0.24	0.02	0.27
	Sum	2.98	1.27	0	–	–	–	–
	C	0.92	0.08	0	150	1.00	0.01	0.44
	P	0.23	0.21	0	90	0.44	0.01	0.13

Table 9.1 (*cont.*)

'Round'	Input	X			z	Dist.* δ	Incr.** γ δ/z	Cum[+] γ
	S	0	0	0	85	0	0	0
(6)	K	0.07	0.15	0	30	0.22	0.01	0.16
	L	0.45	0.23	0	83	0.68	0.01	0.25
	T	0.06	0.08	0	12	0.14	0.01	0.28
	Sum	1.73	0.75	0	–	–	–	–
	C	0.54	0.05	0	150	0.58	0.00	0.44
	P	0.13	0.12	–	90	0.26	0.00	0.13
	S	0	0	0	85	0	0	0
(7)	K	0.04	0.09	0	30	0.13	0.00	0.16
	L	0.26	0.13	0	83	0.39	0.00	0.25
	T	0.03	0.05	0	12	0.08	0.01	0.29
	Sum	1.00	0.44	0	–	–	–	–
	C	0.31	0.03	0	150	0.34	0.00	0.44
	P	0.08	0.07	0	90	0.15	0.00	0.14
	S	0	0	0	85	0	0	0
(8)	K	0.02	0.05	0	30	0.07	0.00	0.17
	L	0.15	0.08	0	83	0.23	0.00	0.25
	T	0.02	0.03	0	12	0.05	0.00	0.30
	Sum	0.58	0.26	0	–	–	–	–
	C	0.19	0.02	0	150	0.20	0.00	0.44
	P	0.04	0.04	0	90	0.09	0.00	0.14
	S	0	0	0	85	0	0	0
(9)	K	0.01	0.03	0	30	0.04	0.00	0.17
	L	0.09	0.04	0	83	0.13	0.00	0.25
	T	0.01	0.02	0	12	0.03	0.00	0.30
	Sum	0.34	0.15	0	–	–	–	–

*Distribution due to suppliers. **Incremental norm. [+]Cumulative norm.

and p_2y_3 lr to the other sectors, respectively. In every case the initial issue will eventually 'settle' in the factor and tax banks and allow the factor-norms to be calculated by simple division.

A full-scale algebraic proof of this would be inordinately lengthy and tedious. Suffice it to say here that it would be based on the resolution of the $Q^{\urcorner}$-term in the definition of factor-norms (8.9) into the infinite geometric series $I + Q + Q^2$ . . . whose separate terms show the successive 'rounds' of the process described.

In Table 9.1 we content ourselves with an arithmetic illustration of the process based on the figures of Chapter 4, which yields the factor-norms 0.17 and 0.25 after nine rounds (the figures are 0.1689 and 0.2536 without rounding) and would approach the true values 0.17 and 0.26 very rapidly if the process were continued, while the cumulative results of 0.44, 0.14, and 0 approach the commodity-norms established in the same exercise.

The 'norm' generated after nine rounds in the 'tax bank' (0.30) would be a factor-norm only if the payments into that bank corresponded to genuine factor contributions rather than mere residuals or rents. The figure must be considered devoid of meaning for the time being.

Note

1 The norm-values that the totality of all factors contributes to each of the end-uses are clearly the element of the row-vector $\acute{w}N'$. But by virtue of (8.9) and (8.7) we have:

$$\acute{w}N' = \acute{w}RQ^{-1}\hat{m} = \acute{\imath}\hat{w}RQ^{-1}\hat{m} = \acute{\imath}WQ^{-1}\hat{m} = \acute{\omega}Q^{-1}\hat{m}.$$

Further, if the list of factors is complete in the sense of exhausting the current value of each product (i.e. if $\acute{\imath}X + \acute{\omega} = \acute{z}Q + \acute{\omega} = \acute{z}$ and therefore $\acute{\omega}Q^{-1} = z$), the above chain of equations may be continued:

$$\acute{w}N' = \acute{\omega}Q^{-1}\hat{m} = \acute{z}\hat{m} = \acute{\imath}\hat{z}\hat{m} = \acute{\imath}\hat{y} = \acute{y}.$$

Thus, the total norm-value of all factors taken together equals the yield y_k of whichever sector k is selected as the use-valuation basis for the computation of norms; i.e.,

$$w_1 n_k^1 + w_2 n_k^2 \ldots + w_m n_k^m = y_k \text{ for all } k = 1, 2 \ldots n.$$

10

EIGENPRICES AND DERIVATIVES – DEFINITION AND ALGEBRA

It is undoubtedly one of the signal achievements of mainstream economics to have overcome the uncomfortable dichotomy between 'value-in-exchange' (cost-based) and 'value-in-use' (utility-based) which Marxian and related systems have to live with. The synthesis of these two archetypal value-forming principles into a single concept of value or competitive price lies at the heart of Marshallian and neoclassical economics as it has been accepted and taught even at the most elementary level (demand and supply) for over a century now. Previous chapters of this book have explored particular approaches to the two principles in turn, culminating in the two statements of (8.10) which elucidate the transmission of costs and utilities from one end of the economy to the other (i.e. from goods to factors and vice versa), and which we repeat here for ease of reference:

$$\acute{p}(f) = \frac{1}{\phi_*}\acute{f}C \text{ and } \acute{n}(p) = \acute{p}N. \tag{10.1}$$

It now remains for us to merge them into a single concept of value reflecting the operation of both principles in equal measure.

What we propose is a simple merging or synthesis of the two principles expressed in (10.1) which, for want of anything better, we shall call the system of 'eigenprices', thus recruiting the German prefix for 'own' or 'proper' which has by now become common international coinage in linear algebra and would appear to claim neither too much nor too little for this new and untried tool of analysis.[1]

Starting from the first equation of (10.1), we note that it defines a transformation or 'mapping' from factor-prices $\acute{f}$ to a correlative set of commodity prices $\acute{p}(f)$. We may now enquire how this resultant set would 'map back' into factor-price space when subjected to the transformation defined by the second equation of (10.1), resulting in $\acute{n}(p)$. To ascertain this we must map f into itself by going through the two stages $\acute{p}(f)$ and $\acute{n}(p)$ in sequence, thus producing

$$\acute{n}\,[\acute{p}(f)] = \acute{n}\left(\frac{1}{\phi_*}fC\right) = \left(\frac{1}{\phi_*}\acute{f}C\right)N = \frac{1}{\phi_*}\acute{f}F, \tag{10.2}$$

where F stands for the 'cost-norm matrix' CN.[2] The result of this reflexive mapping, will in general deviate from $\acute{f}$ unless our initial choice of $\acute{f}$ has hit upon a very particular set known as an 'eigenvector' or 'latent vector' of F. Yet any discrepancy between $\acute{f}$ and $\frac{1}{\phi_*}\acute{f}F$ must be taken as a prima facie inconsistency or derogation from rationality in the factor-price set we have selected: Some or all these prices deviate from the properly valued contributions (norms) of the factors (as derived from the properly costed commodities they produce), and some or all of the commodity-prices deviate from the full costs of the properly normed factors absorbed in their production. In fact, the economy is beset by extra-normal profits or losses for factor-owners and producers implicit in a price system that is distorted by just the sort of 'extra-economic' incubus (monopoly power, extortion, administrative fiat, etc.) which it is the purpose of any rational price-system to eliminate.

A fully consistent and 'rational' factor- and product-price system $(\acute{f}, \acute{p})$ would have to be such that each was the proper mapping of the other as per (10.1) and therefore 'mapped back into itself'; i.e., it would have to satisfy the two equations

$$\acute{f} = \acute{n}(p) = \acute{p}N \text{ and } \acute{p} = \acute{p}(f) = \frac{1}{\phi_*}\acute{f}C \tag{10.3}$$

thus leading to the requirements

$$\acute{f} = \frac{1}{\phi_*}\acute{f}CN \text{ and } \acute{p} = \frac{1}{\phi_*}\acute{p}NC$$

or, equivalently,

$$\acute{f}(\phi_* I - F) = \acute{O} \text{ and } \acute{p}(\phi_* I - P) = \acute{O} \tag{10.4}$$

where F and P stand for the 'cost-norm' and 'norm-cost' matrices CN and NC respectively.[3] To solve these equations in a non-trivial way the scalar ϕ_* must be chosen to make the system's determinant vanish; i.e., it must be an 'eigenvalue' or 'latent root' of the matrices F and P,[4] which makes $\acute{f}$ and $\acute{p}$ into the corresponding eigenvectors of the two matrices, to be known as the 'eigenprices' of the economic system defined by X, Y, and W of scheme (6.1).[5]

Notes

1 Expressions like 'intrinsic', 'implicit', or 'endogenous' probably claim too much for the new concept without necessarily conveying more precise or relevant information.

2 The matrix F will be recognized as the conspectus of the factor-norms of all possible single-yield bases weighted in proportion to the single-factor costs of the base-yield commodities; i.e., its typical element f_r^s will equal $\acute{c}_r \grave{n}^s$ or $c_r^1 n_s^1 + c_r^2 n_s^2 + \ldots$.

3 The first of these (F) is the conspectus of cost-weighted norms (see n. 2) and the second that of norm-weighted costs with every valuation-base featuring as an alternative weighting system in both cases.

4 The requirements of economic sense (reality and non-negativity) imply, moreover, that it is the *dominant* (largest) latent root that must be chosen, along with the latent vector corresponding to it. Given (10.3), it can be shown that the ϕ_* will satisfy both equations of (10.4) since $\acute{f}C$ can be substituted by $\phi_* \acute{p}$ in the first requirement, thus yielding $\phi_* \acute{f} = \phi_* \acute{p} N$, while the second is derived by multiplying both sides by C. Moreover, as long as F is semi-positive and indecomposable the eigenvector f associated with its dominant root ϕ_* is bound to be positive, and therefore all eigenprices $\acute{p}$ are at least non-negative.

5 The use of latent roots and vectors in price analysis is not new. These tools have found application both in the exegesis of classical price systems and in the construction of novel price concepts, and are implicit in some types of value theory conceived long before the mathematics of linear algebra had become 'naturalized' in the discipline of economics. See, also, F. Seton, 'The Transformation Problem', *Review of Economic Studies*, June 1957; and A. Brody, *Proportions, Prices and Planning*, North-Holland Publishing Company, Amsterdam 1970. See also Michio Morishima, 'Marx in the Light of Modern Economic Theory', *Econometrica*, July 1974.

11
EIGENCOST AND EIGENYIELD

11a Definition and meaning

The meaning of the suggested price system can be further clarified by restating the requirements as

$$\acute{p} = \frac{1}{\phi_*}\acute{p}NC = \frac{1}{\phi_*}\acute{f}C = \frac{1}{\phi_*}\acute{f}BA^{\urcorner} \qquad (11.1)$$

where the vector $\acute{f}B$ will be recognized as the eigenprice-value of the primary inputs ('value-added') per unit output of each sector and therefore $\acute{f}BA^{\urcorner}$ as their 'full' (direct and indirect) factor costs, i.e. the value-added by the sectors in terms of the norms $\acute{f}$, which themselves reflect factor scarcities in relation to final demand. The coefficient $1/\phi_*$ thus states the uniform proportion in which these value-added measures must be 'blown-up' to give the eigenprices of the sectoral products, i.e. the uniform *ad valoren* VAT-coefficient. Its reciprocal, ϕ_*, therefore measures the uniform proportion of the eigenprice of products returned to factor-owners after deduction of the notional value-added tax, i.e. the factor-cost ratio of each and every product in terms of eigenprices, to be termed the 'eigencost ratio' of the system. Correlatively, the ratio $\sigma_*(= 1/\phi_* - 1)$ will measure the proportion of eigenprice witheld from the factors of production as such and accruing either to the government in the shape of VAT or as an equivalent unilateral tribute to agents not acting in the capacity of the factors specified in the model (monopoly or extra-normal profit, extortion, or pricing errors by central agencies). This incubus is therefore analogous to the Marxian 'surplus' defined as accruing to capitalists over and above the costs of materials ('constant capital') and labour ('variable capital') that they have to bear, except that our concept of 'eigensurplus' is in no way bound up with a one-factor theory of value or with any notion of class-exploitation.

The analogy becomes even closer when it is recalled that, as in the case of the Marxian surplus, the eigenprices ($\acute{f}$, $\acute{p}$) will ensure the distribution of the incubus among producers in strict proportion to the total factor-cost (value-added) contributed by each, the latter thus playing the same role as Marx's 'variable capital' (wage-costs), from which the 'surplus' is extracted through a uniform 'rate of exploitation' (ϵ). Our eigensurplus ratio σ_*, however, could be identified as exploitation only in so far as it was not channelled through VAT to a government deemed to act in the social interest, but accrued to an 'unproductive' club of sectoral entrepreneurs contributing no factor with a positive 'yield-norm' under the operative system of eigenprices. Even to that extent, however, the victims of this exploitation would not necessarily be wage-earners, and its beneficiaries not necessarily class-bound owners of the means of production. Instead, the beneficiaries would be holders of monopolies or special bargaining power capable of enforcing tariff protection, excessive wage-incomes, extortionate rent or interest, or any other form of uneconomic reward.

It might be more fruitful, however, to look at the ratio σ_* as a measure of the excess value that the system is capable of yielding over and above the necessary rewards of its production factors when properly remunerated (costed) in accordance with their scarcities in relation to final demand. It is in fact in a special sense an indicator of 'cost efficiency' in the exploitation of all specified factors taken together, and thus comes near to a standard of systemic 'merit' in Professor Bergson's sense.[1] It falls short of such a standard, however, as it could attain a high value not merely owing to high factor-productivities in relation to factor-rewards, but also owing to excessive coercive powers exercised by public or private policy-makers in depressing the rewards of some or all productive factors, e.g. by systematic anti-consumptionist policies, or excessive forced investment or defence policies. Nevertheless, as a crucial characteristic of a system's operation which enables unbiased comparisons to be made, the eigensurplus ratio remains an indicator of great interest for the assessment of economic performance. The latent root of the factor-valuation matrix F from which it is derived will be termed the 'eigencost ratio' of the system, as it measures the proportion of disposable value flows which, apart from direct taxation, is returned to the factors as the proper cost for creating that value. It is only the surplus remaining available over and above this which (direct taxation apart) can be used in a discretionary manner according to social policy or need, rather than 'work'. The eigensurplus ratio should therefore also have a certain appeal to Marxist ideologists in spite of its radical departure from their value theories, by assessing – in a thoroughly 'bourgeois' manner, of course – the extent to which a system is able to pass from the 'realm of necessity' to the 'realm of freedom', i.e. from the socialist principle of 'distribution according to work' to the communist prescription of 'distribution according to need'.

If this surplus is to measure the *total* share of GNP diverted to social policy in this manner, the factor contributions W in scheme (6.1) would of course need to be recorded *net* of all direct taxes levied on the factors (income tax, profits tax, corporation tax, etc.). To the extent that they are recorded *gross* of such taxes, the eigenyield will measure only that part of the surplus that is extracted from factor contributions through the operation of the price system, i.e. that part which would be 'automatically' withdrawn from 'distribution according to work' if the correct system of eigenprices were in operation. Additional withdrawals would still be possible, but only by direct public interference in the income stream in the shape of direct taxation or confiscation net of unilateral transfers in the other direction (wage subsidies or family income supplements paid to workers, operating subsidies to companies or individual profit earners, etc.). In practice, the sectoral distribution of such taxes would be extremely difficult to ascertain, and we shall therefore need to content ourselves with the computation of the 'pre-tax eigenyield', which measures the system's capacity for discretionary appropriations without resorting to unilateral transfers of income.

An eigencost ratio below unity (implying a positive eigensurplus) thus betokens some degree of pre-tax alienation or expropriation of the providers of primary inputs in favour of the 'community', 'government', or other beneficiaries (foreign countries, the 'future', etc.). It implies that the economic system is 'more than paying its way'. By contrast, a ratio above unity (i.e. a negative eigensurplus) would imply a degree of subsidization of current factors by non-factor agents, possibly by the government drawing on the past (consuming capital), the future (increasing national debt), or on foreign countries (current external deficit); it characterizes an economic system unable or unwilling to 'pay its way' out of its own resources as becoming available to it here and now, unless it is prepared to depress factor rewards sufficiently by direct taxation. An inter-system comparison of eigensurplus ratios, undertaken with due caution, may therefore be of considerable interest.

Finally, it should be recognized that any quantitative expression for the pre-tax eigensurplus actually computed from a concrete scheme as displayed in (6.1) can only be relative to the 'factor base' specified in that model. It will measure the proportion of economic yield (national income) accruing to *any* agents other than the owners of the specified factors and may therefore include returns to proper factors of production that for one reason or another have had to be omitted from the specified base. Such reasons may be mere lack of statistical data on some factors that are in principle measurable, or conceptual difficulties in the way of measuring others held to be contributing to the productive effort to an unquantifiable extent ('entrepreneurship', 'technical know-how', 'X-efficiency', etc.).

11b Eigensurplus and residual 'inputs'

The eigensurplus as defined above may be interpreted as the eigenvaluation of the residual tax or profit row τ in our basic scheme (6.1), when its components are formally treated as the productive contributions of a notional 'factor' and given a positive eigen-norm g on a par with genuine factors. This may be seen by repeating the algebraic derivation of eigenprices with the south-west (third) quadrant of the basic scheme and all related matrices (W, B, R, $\hat{w}$, etc.) 'augmented' by the row $\acute{\tau}$, now 'annexed' to the normal factor-input rows $\acute{w}$:

$$W_a = \begin{pmatrix} W \\ \acute{\tau} \end{pmatrix}, B_a = W_a \hat{z}^{-1} = \begin{pmatrix} B \\ \acute{\rho} \end{pmatrix}, \hat{w}_a = \begin{pmatrix} \hat{w} & 0 \\ 0 & \tau \end{pmatrix}, R_a = \hat{w}_a^{-1} W_a$$

$$= \begin{pmatrix} R \\ \acute{\tau}/\tau \end{pmatrix}, \quad \text{and } \acute{f}_a = (\acute{f}, g) \tag{11.2}$$

and therefore

$$C_a = B_a \bar{A}^{\rceil} = \begin{pmatrix} C \\ \acute{\rho}\bar{A}^{\rceil} \end{pmatrix}, N_a = \hat{m}\bar{Q}^{\rceil\prime} R_a' = (N, \hat{m}\bar{Q}^{\rceil\prime}\grave{\tau}/\tau).$$

These augmentations transform the matrix F (whose latent root furnishes the 'eigencost-ratio' ϕ_*) into the larger matrix:

$$F_a = C_a N_a = \begin{pmatrix} C \\ \acute{\rho}\bar{A}^{\rceil} \end{pmatrix} (N, \hat{m}\bar{Q}^{\rceil\prime}\grave{\tau}/\tau) = \begin{pmatrix} F & \cdot & \cdot \\ \acute{\rho}\bar{A}^{\rceil}N & \cdot & \cdot \end{pmatrix} \tag{11.3}$$

whose characteristic equation raises the latent root to unity (owing to the inclusion of $\acute{\tau}$ among genuine factor-costs) and defines the new inclusive factor-norms f:

$$\acute{f}_a(I - F_a) = \acute{O} \text{ or } \acute{f}_a = \acute{f}_a F_a; \text{i.e. } [\acute{f}, g] = [\acute{f}, g] \begin{pmatrix} F & \cdot & \cdot \\ \acute{\rho} \bar{A}^{\rceil} N & \cdot & \cdot \end{pmatrix} \tag{11.4}$$

The first element on the right-hand side establishes the equality:

$$\acute{f} = \acute{f}F + g\acute{\rho}\bar{A}^{\rceil}N \text{ or } (1 - \phi_*)\acute{f} = g_*\acute{\rho}\bar{A}^{\rceil}N \tag{11.5}$$

Multiplying both sides of (11.5) by the column-vector of factor-uses $\grave{w}$, we finally obtain:[2]

$$(1 - \phi_*)\acute{f}\grave{w} = g\acute{\rho}\bar{A}^{\rceil}N\grave{w}, \text{ or } (1 - \phi)\acute{f}_*\grave{w} = g_*\acute{\tau}\bar{A}^{\rceil}N\grave{w} = g_*\tau. \tag{11.6}$$

The last statement, which assumes standarized norming, shows clearly that the eigensurplus, expressed here as the proportion $(1 - \phi_*)$ of national income (in eigenprices), equals the sum of residuals $\acute{\tau}$ valued at their standardized norm g_* as it emerges from their treatment as the contributions of a notional productive factor.

This demonstration clarifies an important point, so far only implicit in our argument. The existence of the eigensurplus in our interpretation of the term is conditional on the existence of a genuine residual row $\acute{\tau}$ not attributable to any of the productive factors specified in the basic scheme.[3] This in turn precludes the measurement of any factor-inputs $\acute{w}_r$ (e.g. profits) as a mere residual, since this would by definition banish all non-factor residuals from the economy, unless these were identified with taxes or subsidies included in the prices of commodities.

11c Dimensional balance and invariance

The identity uncovered in the last section may help to solve a disturbing conundrum. The definition of factor-norms by means of the matrix $N(= \hat{m}Q^{\rceil\prime}R')$ may create the impression that, contrary to the 'productivity' dimension (glr/flr) that our interpretation of Section 9a implies, their formally established dimension was that of *pure numbers* (/.), given that the constituent matrices ($\hat{m}$, $Q^{\rceil}$, and R) are all composed of 'quotas' (i.e. proportions or pure ratios). A brief look at footnote 1 of that chapter, however, should convince us that, given the accounting identity between row and column sums in scheme (6.1), secured by the 'assimilation' of the residuals $\acute{\tau}$ to the list of genuine factor-inputs $\acute{w}$, the matrix $Q^{\rceil}$ takes on the alternative formal dimension glr/flr, which it then transfers to the factor-norms N. This is so by virtue of the fact that the identity $\acute{z}Q + \acute{\omega} = \acute{z}$ implies the relationship $\acute{\omega}Q^{\rceil} = \acute{z}$, in which $\acute{\omega}$ and $\acute{z}$ clearly have dimensions flr and glr, respectively.

The same accounting identity and assimilation of surplus establishes the invariance of the eigenyield $\sigma_*(1/\phi_* - 1)$ to variations in commodity and factor units, *so long as these variations leave the accounting identity undisturbed*; for such variations will merely transform the F-matrix into a 'similar' matrix F_* pre-multiplied by the diagonal of factor-unit variations (say $\hat{u}$) and post-divided by the same diagonal (i.e. post-multiplied by $\hat{u}^{-1}$), regardless of the variations in commodity units (say $\hat{v}$), thus leaving the latent roots of F (eigenvalues) unaffected.

We can maintain our dimensional interpretation of the factor-norms perhaps most easily by reflecting that flr and glr are after all no less commensurable than the glr of different goods (say coal-lira and power-lira) or the flr of different factors (say labour-lira and capital-lira), and that for our purposes we may equate them to a single form of undifferentiated 'lira', to be regarded as the measure of a 'physical unit' of *anything* of economic value, whether commodity or factor. In that case the productivity of a factor could be expressed as so many *physical* units (of final product) per *physical* unit (of the factor), thus reducing to a pure number or ratio by construction. By the same token, of course, our working hypothesis would re-interpret the commodity costs of matrix C as pure numbers.

Uncomfortable though this conclusion may be, it should be borne in mind that many forms of input–output exercises conducted in terms of 'constant money prices' with implicit accounting identities in undifferentiated currencies fall into similar ambiguities, even though they fail to make them explicit. At any rate, our working hypothesis should enable us to interpret commodity prices p and factor-norms n as unit-costs and unit-productivities respectively by attributing to them either the dimension of pure numbers or those of flr/glr and glr/flr respectively, as the context may dictate. The former attribution helps us demonstrate the dimensional balance of our procedure, while the latter aids our intuitive understanding of its purport.

Notes

1 Abram Bergson, *Productivity and the Social System – the USSR and the West*, Harvard University Press, Cambridge, Mass., 1978.

2 By virtue of footnote 1 of Chapter 9 we have $N\grave{w} = \grave{y}$, and therefore $\acute{\rho}A^{\urcorner}N\grave{w} = \acute{\rho}A^{\urcorner}\grave{y} = \acute{\rho}\grave{z}$ (see 6.7). Finally, from the definition of $\acute{\rho}$ as $\acute{\tau}\grave{z}^{-1}$, it follows that $\acute{\rho}\grave{z} = \acute{\tau}\grave{\imath} = \tau$.

3 I am indebted to Mr M. FG. Scott of Nuffield College for alerting me to the need to enter this caveat.

12

THE 'SCALING' OF EIGENPRICES

Equations (10.4), which define the system of eigenprices of products and factors ($\acute{p}$, $\acute{f}$), identify them as the dominant eigenvectors of the matrices P and F. As is well known, however, eigenvectors are defined only up to a multiplicative constant. In fact, we have merely defined the *structure* or scale-model of eigenprices, without as yet specifying their absolute values of 'scale'. This absolute scaling is bound to be arbitrary and can follow any of a number of principles, such as keeping certain aggregates or ratios of the current-price tableau invariant to revaluation.[1] We might for instance fix the scale so that the total eigensurplus comes to equal the current value of a residual 'tax'-row, in line with some notion that revaluation in eigenprices ought merely to 'redistribute' the surplus without altering its size. The macro-aggregate we have chosen to keep invariant to the transformation in the present exercise, however, is the sum of all yields supplied by the industrial sectors of (6.1), in fact the GNP $y_0 (= \Sigma y)$. This has the advantage of yielding eigenprices with a weighted mean equal to unity,[2] thus making them more readily comparable with current prices (= 1) by simply noting their deviations from that mean.

Scaled in this way, we call the eigenprices 'standardized' and denote them by (p_*, f_*). Their reciprocals, which measure current prices per unit-worth of eigenprice, will thus enable us to spot relative 'undervaluations' ($1/p_* < 1$) or 'overvaluations' ($1/p_* > 1$) of products or factors by the current price system with the greatest ease. In the same way, the eigenrentals would emerge 'standardized' to replicate the factor-costed national income; i.e.

$$\acute{f}_* \grave{w} = \phi_* y_0 .$$

When the original tableau (6.1) is thus 'transformed' by the revaluation of each and every flow in standardized eigenprices (denoted by appending a subscript asterisk to symbols: y_*, w_*, z_*, etc.), we can use it for the comparison of important structural ratios (investment ratios, foreign trade dependence, factor shares, or branch contributions to GNP) across different systems, as has been done in Part III below, without the need to impose alien or arbitrarily chosen price structures on the systems to be compared. The standardized eigenprices implicit in each system provide us with an objectively determined yardstick independent of those arbitrary choices to which the results of comparisons are so often unduly and notoriously sensitive.

It must be stressed, however, that, given the inevitable arbitrariness remaining in the 'scaling-factor', the *absolute* eigenvalues of economic flows still cannot serve as a basis for inter-system comparison, unless we are prepared to indulge in some form of 'price-grafting', such as the initial acceptance of universally valid world prices for some or all final products and the derivation from them of internal factor-norms and product costings leading to 'shadow prices' for both traded and non-traded goods and factors, in partial conformity with certain prescriptions relating to project appraisal in developing countries.[3] This, however, is a possible application of eigenprice calculations whose legitimacy and results are beyond the scope of this book and remain to be explored elsewhere.

Notes

1 The analogous problem in the context of Marxian values and 'production prices' is discussed more exhaustively in F. Seton, 'The Transformation Problem', *Review of Economic Studies*, vol. 24, 1956/57.

2 $p_* \grave{y} = \acute{\imath} \grave{y} = y_0$ implies $\acute{p} (\grave{y} / y_0) = 1$.

3 See Ian M. D. Little and James A. Mirrlees, *Manual of Industrial Project Analysis in Developing Countries*, vols. I and II, Development Centre of OECD, Paris, 1969.

13

A METHOD FOR GENERATING EIGENPRICES AND COST RATIOS

The definition of eigenprices (10.4) readily suggests a procedure for generating them by a process of iterative adjustment starting from an initial market-based or freely chosen price system in any economy.

Based on the initial list of factor-prices $\acute{f}_0$, we allow the normal ('cost-generating') money circulation to generate the correlative factor-costs (ex-profit) of commodities in the 'first-round', i.e. $\acute{p}_1 = \acute{f}_0 C$. We then accept these as the basis of a new round of 'norm-generating' circulation, distributing goods-lira accordingly to final users and instructing economic agents to behave as described in Section 9b. This will generate the revised factor-norms of the first round $\acute{f}_1 = \acute{p}_1 N$. These are then accepted as the charges per unit factor in a second round of commodity-costing circulation. The process of alternating 'norm- and cost-generating' circulations must then be continued indefinitely, leading to successive revisions of norms from those of the previous round:

$$\acute{f}_{r+1} = \acute{p}_{r+1} N = \acute{f}_r CN = \acute{f}_r F$$

until the revised norms assume a stable proportionate structure, no longer subject to significant revision in further rounds; i.e.,

$$\lim_{r \to R} \acute{f}_{r+1} = \phi_* \acute{f}_r$$

i.e. until

$$\acute{f}_R (\phi_* I - F) = \acute{0}. \qquad (13.1)$$

When this point has been reached, the norms of the latest round are sufficient approximations to the eigenprices of factors, and the constant proportionality factor ϕ approaches the eigencost ratio of the system. As the signal that this has been substantially achieved, we

Table 13.1 *The generation of eigenprices**

'Round' r	$\acute{f}_r = \acute{p}_r N$		$\acute{p}_{r+1} = \acute{f}_r C$			$\acute{\phi} = \acute{f}_{r+1} \hat{f}_r^{1}$	
0	0.5	2	1.49	1.19	1.49	–	–
1	1.43	1.47	1.27	1.19	1.36	2.86	0.74
2	1.31	1.33	1.15	1.08	1.23	0.92	0.90
3	1.19	1.20	1.04	0.98	1.11	0.91	0.90
4	1.07	1.09	0.94	0.89	1.01	0.90	0.91
5	0.97	0.99	0.86	0.81	0.92	0.91	0.91
.	.	.	.	.	.	.	.
.	.	.	.	.	.	.	.
.	.	.	.	.	.	.	.
f, ϕ	1	1	0.87	0.82	0.93	0.91	

*Non-standardized eigenprices of Chapter 5 before profit.

may accept the convergence of the 'revision ratios' $\acute{f}_{r+1} \hat{f}_r^{1}$ to a single figure, ϕ_*.

Table 13.1 shows the result of alternating 'norm- and cost-generating circulations' applied to the figures of Chapter 5, with initial factor-prices set at 0.5 and 2 glr per lira of capital and labour respectively. As can be seen, a close approximation to the correct (non-standardized) eigenprices and eigencost ratio is attained in as few as five rounds.

The same result could be achieved by starting from any other initial system of factor or goods-prices – notably from actual market-prices for final goods ($\acute{p}_0 = \acute{i}$), although a latent root as close to unity as we have assumed may in some instances slow down or obfuscate the process of convergence, or even cause the ratios in the last two columns to show self-reversing discrepancies (0.89, 0.93, followed by 0.93, 0.89 etc.) for many successive rounds before ultimately settling down to equality. This, however, affects only the efficacy of the process of generating eigenprices proposed here, and not the basic principles underlying their definition.

PART II

Eigenprices: Historical Parallels, Special Cases, and Extensions

14
THE PRODUCTION OF COMMODITIES BY MEANS OF PRIMARY FACTORS ONLY ('FEEDBACK-FREE' MODELS)

The classical models in use before input–output analysis burst on the scene, and still in the minds of economists for most theoretical purposes, dispense with intersectoral feedback effects and treat the production process as a direct transformation of primary (non-produced) inputs into final commodities. What happens to our eigen-prices and related concepts in such a 'degenerate subsystem'?

The formal modification required is the reduction of the inter-sectoral coefficient and quota matrices to zero – i.e., $A = Q = 0$ – and the consequent reduction of their Leontief inverses to the unit matrix – i.e., $\overline{A}\rceil = \overline{Q}\rceil = I$, – with the diagonal matrix of end-use quotas $\hat{m}(= \hat{z}^{-1}\hat{y})$ similarly reduced to I. This simplifies both 'cost-' and 'norm-' matrices as defined in (7.4) and (8.9) to[1]

$$C = B \quad \text{and} \quad N = M' \equiv R'. \tag{14.1}$$

Not surprisingly, therefore, the full costs reduce to direct costs and the 'yield-norms' to factor-quotas; i.e., the yield-product of every factor in terms of a given product becomes simply its allocation to that product, and its 'yield-productivity' the proportion (quota) of the factor so allocated. Accordingly, the factor-valuation ('cost-norm') matrix defined in (10.2) becomes

$$F = BM'. \tag{14.2}$$

The eigencost ratio is thus the eigenvalue of all possible quota-weightings $\acute{b}^r \grave{m}^j$ or $\acute{m}_j \grave{b}^r$ (with r taking on all factor-, and j all product-labels).

In particular, if the number of sectors (but not necessarily factors) is reduced to one, the sectoral allocation quotas of every factor, and therefore all norms, will trivially rise to unity; i.e., the average (and marginal) physical product becomes one.[2] In these conditions the factor quota matrix M' reduces to the all-unit vector $\acute{i}$, while the factor-coefficient matrix B turns into the column vector $\grave{b}$. In consequence, the factor-valuation matrix F (10.2) becomes a 'dyadic' matrix $\grave{b}\acute{i}$ whose eigenvector and dominant eigenvalue can be shown to be $\acute{i}$ and $\acute{i}\grave{b}$ respectively

$$\acute{i}(\acute{i}\grave{b}I - \grave{b}\acute{i}) = (\acute{i}\grave{b} - \acute{i}\grave{B})\acute{i} = 0. \qquad (14.3)$$

The latter ($\acute{i}\grave{b}$) is of course the reduced system's 'eigencost ratio' ϕ (10.2), thus shown to be the simple sum of all factor input-coefficients – or the single coefficient b, if we drive trivialization to the extreme of reducing also the number of factors to one. We have thus established that, in the traditional one-good–one-factor model, our 'eigencost ratio' is represented by the single input-requirement per unit output, and the 'eigensurplus ratio' σ correspondingly by the expression $1/b - 1$, i.e. the excess of output per unit input over the factor's marginal productivity (its due reward). This result, trivial though it is, accords well with our intuitive understanding of the more complex general scheme.

We can, however, get little or no help from this particular model for a better understanding of eigenprices themselves; for the model trivializes these out of existence by positing a world in which marginal costs (in terms of all factors) and marginal products are all identically equal to one. It follows that *any* commodity price we may choose will equate the marginal revenue products of all factors to that one price and at the same time ensure that it also measures the commodity's marginal cost, once the factors are all equally priced. The 'principle of reciprocal marginality' (PRM), i.e. self-consistent product and factor-pricing in conformity with marginal costs and marginal revenue productivities respectively, is therefore automatically operative in this model at current prices, and we need not do any repricing to achieve it.[3]

We fare somewhat better in this respect when we turn to the alternative non-feedback model characterized by a single factor serving the production of n different goods. Here it is best to start by expressing the product prices p with the aid of the norm-cost matrix P as per (10.4). The latter can be obtained by commuting the matrix factors in product (14.2); i.e.

$$P = M'B \qquad (14.4)$$

which under the assumptions of the model reduces to the dyadic matrix $\grave{m}\acute{b}$. By analogy with (14.3), the eigenvector and dominant eigenvalue of this can be shown to be $\acute{b}$ and $\acute{b}\grave{m}$ respectively:

$$\acute{b}(\acute{b}\grave{m}I - \grave{m}\acute{b}) = (\acute{b}\grave{m} - \acute{b}\grave{m})\acute{b} = \acute{0}. \tag{14.5}$$

Thus the eigencost ratio ϕ is now the weighted mean of the input-coefficients $\acute{b}$ (with the end-use quotas for weights), while the eigen-prices of the products become identical with their direct factor require-ments per unit (marginal costs). The eigenprice of the factor (f) can then be chosen at will, provided only that the n products are priced at $f\acute{b}$. In this case, therefore, the principle of reciprocal marginality is not realized by the current price structure, since the marginal costs of products (in terms of the single factor) are no longer unity, but equal to their factor requirements per unit (multiplied by the factor-price f). The two 'halves' of the 'Principle of Reciprocal Marginality' (see next chapter) could be stated explicitly as

(1) $\acute{p}$ to be = marginal cost (including mark-up) $= \dfrac{1}{\phi_*} f\acute{b}$

(2) f to be = marginal revenue-product $= \acute{p}\grave{m}$,

whence $\phi_* \acute{p} = \acute{p}\grave{m}\acute{b}$ or $\acute{p}(\phi_* I - \grave{m}\acute{b}) = \acute{O}$, as stated before.

Notes

1 As the reader will notice, we denote the basic matrices in feedback-free models by the letters immediately preceding in the alphabet those of the full models.

2 This trivial result becomes obvious when it is recalled that the physical unit of both product and factor is defined in dollar terms; i.e., \$1 worth of each factor adds \$1 worth to the product, since inputs and outputs must have the same total dollar value.

3 In other words, any system of uniform prices (per dollar's worth) for product and factors can serve as an eigenprice system, including the all-unit vector $\acute{i}$, i.e. the current price system itself.

15

THE LINK WITH MARGINAL ANALYSIS – A LINEAR PROGRAMMING APPROACH

We can now begin to throw a bridge to the more traditional marginalist theory of value by sketching out a possible derivation of full cost and use-norm prices as dual solutions of standard linear programming problems.[1]

Given a set of n final demands $\grave{y}$ and m factor-prices $\acute{f}$, the 'production problem' is the task of choosing the cheapest factor-mix $\grave{w}$ to produce a final bill of goods that is 'sufficient' in the sense of not falling short of the final demand that the community is known to be making on any of the n sectors; i.e.,

$$\min_{w} \acute{f}\grave{w} \text{ subject to } \grave{w} > C\grave{y}. \tag{15.1}$$

The 'dual' of this – the 'marketing problem' – would be the one facing a trader offering to sell the community its desired assortment of products $\grave{y}$ at the most lucrative set of product prices ($\acute{c}$) that is 'realistic' in the sense of not implying a higher charge for any product than the cost of the factor-mix necessary to produce it: i.e.,

$$\max_{c} \acute{c}\grave{y} \text{ subject to } \acute{c} < \acute{f}C. \tag{15.2}$$

The primal and dual constraints may be condensed into the single statement

$$\acute{c}\grave{y} < \acute{f}C\grave{w} < \acute{f}\grave{w} \tag{15.3}$$

and since the first and last terms of this inequality must reach their upper and lower limits respectively, the two problems will be solved simultaneously only when all three terms of (15.3) are equal, and in particular only when

$$\acute{f}C\grave{w} = \acute{c}\grave{y}.$$

A sufficient condition for this to hold is clearly that

$$\acute{c} = \acute{f}C$$

i.e. that, given the factor-prices $\acute{f}$, the product-prices charged be equal to the 'cost-prices' as defined in (7.5). As is well-known, however, the dual solutions of a linear programming problem measure the improvements achievable in the primal objective function (at optimum) by relaxing each of the primal constraints in turn. The cost-prices $\acute{c}$ are thereby shown to be the factor-cost savings obtainable from lowering the final demand for each commodity by one unit – in other words, they are the 'marginal costs' of the products under the conditions assumed.

To find a similar linear programming approach to the factor-norms $\acute{n}$, we must recast the primal–dual pair of programs by shifting from the original to what might be called the 'conjugate' problem.[2] The pre-established data are now product-prices $\acute{p}$ and factor availabilities $\grave{w}$, and a 'supply problem' may be defined as the task of selecting the most valuable final output-mix $\grave{y}$ that is 'feasible' in the sense of requiring no more than the factor-endowments available; i.e.,

$$\max_{y} \acute{p}\grave{y} \text{ subject to } \grave{y} < N\grave{w}. \tag{15.4}$$

The dual to this, which might be called the 'take-over' problem, would be to find the most economic purchase prices for the factors ($\acute{n}$) that are 'acceptable' in the sense of offering no less for any factor combination than the price of the product that could be produced with its aid; i.e.,

$$\min_{n} \acute{n}\grave{w} \text{ subject to } \acute{n} > \acute{p}N. \tag{15.5}$$

At optimum, the two objective functions must again come up fully to the constraints, for which a sufficient condition will evidently be

$$\acute{n} = \acute{p}N$$

thus revealing our use-norms (8.9) as the increases in the primal objective function ($\acute{p}\grave{y}$) achievable by adding extra units to each of the factor endowments $\grave{w}$, in fact as the marginal revenue productivities of the factors.

With full-cost product pricing thus leading us from factor-rentals to marginal product-costs and full-price factor costing from product-prices to marginal factor productivities, it will be clear that our eigenprices, which lead from either to the other and back again, will represent the unique price structure that fulfils the double condition (1) that all factor-rentals equal marginal revenue productivities (in terms of product-prices), and (2) that all product-prices equal marginal costs (in terms of factor-rentals), thus obeying what might be called the 'Principle of Reciprocal Marginality' (PRM) and justifying their characterization as 'quasi-competitive'. The operational meaning and application of PRM is spelled out in somewhat greater detail in the next chapter.

Notes

1 We have not so far succeeded in formulating the primal–dual pairs (15.1)/(15.2) and (15.4)/(15.5) in precise confirmity with the standard paradigms. Their exact nature and mutural relationship is therefore still in doubt, and must be left to mathematical friends and critics for verification as unfinished business. However, intuition and the 'conical' character of the sets involved (in the sense of positive homogeneity of degree one) encourage us to stand by the interpretation offered with some degree of confidence. We are greatly indebted to Professor Terence Gorman of Nuffield College for impressing on us the need to enter this caveat, but wish to exempt him from any responsibility for the way in which we have interpreted it in this footnote.

2 i.e., from the 'input-planning/output-pricing' scheme to the 'output-planning/input-pricing' problem.

16

THE LINK WITH MARGINAL ANALYSIS – THE PRINCIPLE OF RECIPROCAL MARGINALITY GENERALIZED

The Principle of Reciprocal Marginality (PRM) explained at the end of Chapter 15 can be extended from the Leontief model governed by limitational input-coefficients to the general case of non-linear production and transformation functions as used or implied in traditional neoclassical economics. Here the link between output-mix $\grave{z}$ and input-use $\grave{w}$ is provided by functions of the general form

$$t(\grave{z}, \grave{w}) = b \text{ (constant)}$$

whose number could be smaller than that of products (n) or factors (m). If the number is equal to m, the functions could in general be made explicit with respect to each w_j in turn, thus specifying a fixed requirement for each factor deriving solely from the output-mix $\grave{z}$ and independent of the quantities of other factors used. If the number is below m, on the other hand, there is some scope for factor substitution. In what follows we shall allow the maximum scope for this by positing only one such transformation function, assumed sufficient to specify all possible input- and output-mixes in the sense that, given $\grave{w}$, any output-mix $\grave{z}$ obeying $t = b$ could be produced, and, given $\grave{z}$, any factor-mix $\grave{w}$ obeying $t = b$ would be sufficient to produce it.

The first PRM condition – that inputs be priced in accordance with their marginal revenue productivities – can then be formulated by computing the maximal sales revenue obtainable at given product-prices $\acute{p}$ and factor-endowments $\grave{w}$, i.e. by solving the constrained extremal problem

$$\max_{z} s \equiv \acute{p}\grave{z}, \text{ subject to } t(\grave{z}, \grave{w}) = b.$$

The maximizing $\grave{z}$ obtained by standard Lagrangean methods, say $\grave{\zeta}(\acute{p}, \grave{w})$, when substituted in the sales function

$$\acute{p}\grave{\zeta}(\acute{p}, \grave{w})$$

furnish what has in a different context been called the 'maximum-value' or 'indirect-utility' function of the system $\hat{s}$,[1] and the condition requires that the factor rentals $\acute{f}$ be equated to the derivatives of this function with respect to w_j; i.e.,

$$f_j = \frac{\partial \hat{s}}{\partial w_j}(\acute{p}), \quad \text{for} \quad j = 1, 2, \ldots, m \quad \text{or} \quad \acute{f} = \hat{s}_w(\acute{p}).$$

This provides the nonlinear transformation rules for n product-prices into m factor-rentals corresponding to the linear transformation of prices into 'norms' in equation (8.9) which we have called the 'upstream transformation'.

To formulate the corresponding 'downstream transformation' we need only remind ourselves of the 'conjugate' problem of finding the cheapest factor-mix $\grave{w}$ to satisfy the given demand-structure $\grave{z}$; i.e.,

$$\min_w e = \acute{f}\grave{w}, \text{subject to } t(\grave{z}, \grave{w}) = b.$$

Again, the minimizing $\grave{w}$, say $\grave{\omega}(\acute{f}, \grave{z})$, can be obtained by standard Lagrangean methods and substituted in e, to furnish the so-called 'expenditure function',[2] to be renamed more appropriately the 'minimum expenditure function':

$$\check{e} = \acute{f}\grave{\omega}(\acute{f}, \grave{z})$$

whose derivatives (with respect to $\grave{z}$) will in turn furnish the 'downstream' transformation rules (or second PRM conditions)

$$p_i = \frac{1}{\phi_*}\frac{\partial \check{e}}{\partial z_i}(\acute{f}), \quad \text{for} \quad i = 1, 2, \ldots, n \quad \text{or} \quad \acute{p} = \acute{\check{e}}_z(\acute{f})$$

corresponding to the linear transformation (7.6).

If the two sets of transformations applied in series (i.e. the 'reflexive transformation') possess a fixed point, that point is the vector of eigenrentals and eigenprices we are looking for; i.e., the eigenrentals are the solutions $\acute{f}$ of

$$\acute{f} = \acute{\hat{s}}_w\left[\frac{1}{\phi_*}\acute{\check{e}}_z(\acute{f})\right]$$

a system of m equations in $m + 1$ unknowns $(\acute{f}, \phi)$ whose consistency can be assured by the proper choice of ϕ. Simultaneously, the eigenprices of products $\acute{p}$ will emerge from

$$\acute{p} = \frac{1}{\phi_*} \frac{\partial \check{e}}{\partial z_i} [\hat{s}_w (\acute{p})]$$

in the same way.

The generalization we have proposed furnishes the clue to what is perhaps the most illuminating interpretation of the concept of eigenprices. These prices invert the conceptual train of thought of Paretian economics, which leads from given prices and rentals to optimal quantity-mixes (maximizing utility/revenue and minimizing costs), by starting out from quantity-mixes (as observed in input–output flows) and leading to the price and rental systems which must have served as the underlying price base to yield these flows as the outcome of Pareto-optimizing behaviour (i.e. equating marginal revenues to factor-rentals and marginal costs to product-prices). In other words, eigenprices could be thought of as the view that an economy must implicitly be taking of the values of its products and resources for it to have combined them in the observed quantities in pursuit of a Pareto optimum.

The concept would of course be invalidated if it were shown that an economy had systematically or on principle rejected such optima in favour of output- and/or input-combinations that suited its aspirations and endowments less well than could have been achieved. Short of this, however, eigenprices should reflect the economy's own implicit view of the relative urgency of wants and scarcity of resources which informs its activities, and the structural and performance ratios measured in these terms must by that token appraise relative effort, sacrifice, or benefit from the angle of most relevance to those who operate it or suffer under its sway.

Notes

1 See, e.g., A. Dixit, *Optimization in Economic Theory*, Oxford University Press, 1976, pp. 24 *et seq*., and W. M. Gorman, 'Tricks with Utility Functions', in M. Artis and R. Nobay (eds), *Essays in Economic Analysis*, Cambridge University Press, 1976, pp. 211 *et seq*.

2 See Dixit, op. cit., or Gorman op. cit.

17

THE LINK WITH MARGINAL ANALYSIS – A DETAILED APPLICATION OF THE PRM TO TWO-BY-TWO MODELS

We can make this procedure considerably more explicit in the simplified context of a two-factor, two-commodity world, with outputs x, y, and factor-inputs u, v, constrained by a single transformation function

$$t(x, y; u, v) = b.$$

To avoid cumbersome suffixes we shall denote the two commodity prices by p and q, and the factor-rentals by f and g, respectively, reserving the accented letters $\acute{p}$ and $\acute{f}$ for the corresponding two-dimensional vectors.

Our first task is then to establish the 'upstream' transformation by choosing x and y so as to maximize the sales function subject to the given constraint; i.e., in Lagrangean terms,

$$\max_{\lambda, x, y} px + qy - \lambda[t(x, y; u, v) - b]. \tag{17.1}$$

The well-known first-order conditions[1] will then be:

$$\begin{aligned} t &= b \\ \lambda t_x &= p \\ \lambda t_y &= q \end{aligned} \tag{17.2}$$

and the maximizing values of the variables, $\hat{x}$ and $\hat{y}$, could be deduced to furnish the 'maximum-value function' $\hat{s}(= p\hat{x} + q\hat{y})$ in its dependence on the parameters b, p, and q and the input-variables u and v. Its derivatives would then furnish the basis for the upstream transformation which determines the correlative factor-rentals f and g as the marginal productivities $\hat{s}_u$ and $\hat{s}_v$.

Such a procedure, however, would require an explicit specification of the transformation function, necessitating radical departures from generality, and a solution having application only to our arbitrary choice of function.

The need for this can be bypassed by utilizing the equilibrium conditions governing the optimal productivities x_u, x_v and y_u, y_v as imposed by the constraints and the second-order derivatives of the transformation function. Taking total derivatives, on the left-hand sides we find by virtue of the chain-rule:

$$\begin{aligned} t_x x_u + t_y y_u + t_u &= 0 \\ t_x \lambda_u/\lambda + t_{xx} x_u + t_{xy} y_u + t_{xu} &= 0 \\ t_u \lambda_u/\lambda + t_{yx} x_u + t_{yy} y_u + t_{yu} &= 0. \end{aligned} \tag{17.3}$$

Denoting the bordered Hessian and its partitions by ${}^{\ulcorner}H$; H, $\acute{r}$, $\acute{s}$, X, etc., this can be written:

$${}^{\ulcorner}H \begin{Bmatrix} \lambda_u/\lambda \\ x_u \\ y_u \\ 1 \\ 0 \end{Bmatrix} = \left(\begin{array}{c|cc|cc} 0 & t_x & t_y & t_u & t_v \\ \hline t_x & t_{xx} & t_{xy} & t_{xu} & t_{xv} \\ t_y & t_{yx} & t_{yy} & t_{yu} & t_{yv} \\ \hline t_u & t_{ux} & t_{uy} & t_{uu} & t_{uv} \\ t_v & t_{vx} & t_{vy} & t_{vu} & t_{vv} \end{array}\right) \begin{Bmatrix} \lambda_u/\lambda \\ \hline x_u \\ y_u \\ \hline 1 \\ 0 \end{Bmatrix}$$

$$\equiv \left(\begin{array}{c|c|c} 0 & \acute{r} & \acute{s} \\ \hline \grave{r} & X & Y \\ \hline \grave{s} & W & Z \end{array}\right) \begin{Bmatrix} \grave{X}_u \\ \grave{i}_1 \end{Bmatrix} \equiv \grave{0}$$

$$\equiv \left(\begin{array}{c|c} 0 & \acute{t} \\ \hline \grave{t} & H \end{array}\right) \begin{Bmatrix} \lambda_u/\lambda \\ \hline \grave{x}_u \\ \grave{i}_1 \end{Bmatrix}$$

$$\equiv \left(\begin{array}{c|c} {}^{\ulcorner}X & \grave{Y} \\ \hline {}^{\ulcorner}W & Z \end{array}\right) \begin{Bmatrix} \grave{X}_u \\ \hline \grave{i}_1 \end{Bmatrix} \tag{17.4}$$

where $\grave{X}_u$ stands for the 'augmented' vector of marginal productivities

$[\lambda_u/\lambda,\ x_u,\ y_u]'$ and $\grave{i}_1$ for the first column vector of the 2×2 unit matrix.

The matrix equation can easily be solved for $\grave{X}_u$, writing

$$\ulcorner\!XX_u + \grave{Y}\grave{i}_1 = 0, \quad \text{and} \quad \grave{X}_u = -\ulcorner\!X^{-1}Y\grave{i}_1. \tag{17.5}$$

By analogy with (17.3), the marginal productivities of factor v (x_v and y_v) could have been obtained in the same way, except for the substitution of $\grave{i}_2$ for the $\grave{i}_1$-partition of the solution-vector in (17.4), which would have replaced (17.5) by

$$\grave{X}_v = \begin{pmatrix} \lambda_v/\lambda \\ x_v \\ y_v \end{pmatrix} = \begin{pmatrix} \lambda_v/\lambda \\ \grave{x}_v \end{pmatrix} = -\ulcorner\!X^{-1}Y\grave{i}_2. \tag{17.6}$$

The two crucial derivatives of the maximum-value function could therefore be conveniently displayed as the last elements of the vector

$$\begin{aligned} \acute{F} &\equiv [0,\ f,\ g] \\ &= [0,\ \hat{s}_u,\ \hat{s}_v] = [0,\ p,\ q] \begin{pmatrix} 0 & \lambda_u/\lambda & \lambda_v/\lambda_v \\ \grave{0} & x_u & \grave{x}_v \end{pmatrix} \\ &\equiv -\acute{P}(0,\ \ulcorner\!X^{-1}Y) \end{aligned} \tag{17.7}$$

which enables us to write the upstream transformation 'augmented' by dummy zero cyphers in the two variable vectors, i.e.

$$\begin{aligned} \acute{F} \equiv [0,\ f,\ g] &= -[0,\ p,\ q] \cdot -(0,\ \ulcorner\!X^{-1}Y) \\ &\equiv -\acute{P} \cdot - \begin{pmatrix} 0 & \acute{m} \\ \grave{0} & \bar{M} \end{pmatrix} \end{aligned} \tag{17.8}$$

or, more concisely,

$$\acute{F} = \acute{P}\ulcorner\!M^{+}$$

where $\ulcorner\!M^{+}$ has been named by analogy with (8.9) replacing N by M in line with the feedback-free character of the model, and is identical with the 3×3 matrix $-(\grave{0},\ \ulcorner\!X^{-1}\bar{Y})$.

The correlative 'downstream' transformation can be established by minimizing the expenditure function $e(=fu + gv)$ with respect to the factor-inputs u and v, under the t-constraint already assumed, thus minimizing the Lagrangean

$$\min_{\mu, u, v} fu + gv - \mu[t(x, y; u, v) - b]. \tag{17.9}$$

The first-order conditions are now:

$$\begin{aligned} t &= b \\ \mu t_u &= f \\ \mu t_v &= g \end{aligned} \tag{17.10}$$

and the equilibrium conditions governing the optimal marginal costs u_x, u_y and v_x, v_y assume the form

$$\begin{aligned} t_u u_x + t_v v_x + t_x &= 0 \\ t_u \mu_x/\mu + t_{uu} u_x + t_{uv} v_x + t_{ux} &= 0 \\ t_v \mu_x/\mu + t_{vu} u_x + t_{vv} v_x + t_{vx} &= 0 \end{aligned} \tag{17.11}$$

These equations correspond to the upstream transformation based on (17.4) with the rows and columns of the Hessian permuted:

$$\begin{pmatrix} 0 & \acute{s} & \acute{r} \\ \grave{s} & Z & W \end{pmatrix} \begin{Bmatrix} \grave{U}_x \\ \grave{i}_1 \end{Bmatrix} = \grave{0} \tag{17.12}$$

where $\grave{U}_x$ stands for the augmented vector of marginal costs $[\mu_x/\mu, u_x, v_x]$. The marginal costs of the second commodity $\grave{U}_y$, equal to $[\mu_y/\mu, u_y, v_y]$, will evidently need to fulfil the conditions

$$\begin{pmatrix} 0 & \acute{s} & \acute{r} \\ \grave{s} & Z & W \end{pmatrix} \begin{Bmatrix} \grave{U}_y \\ \grave{i}_2 \end{Bmatrix} = \grave{0} \tag{17.13}$$

thus defining the derivatives of the minimal expenditure function as

$$[0, \breve{e}_x, \breve{e}_y] = [0, f, g](\grave{0}, \grave{U}_x, \grave{U}_y) = \acute{F}(\grave{0}, \overline{Z}^{-1}W) \tag{17.14}$$

where $\overline{Z}$ and $\overline{W}$ are the bordered Hessian partitions

$$\begin{pmatrix} 0 & \acute{s} \\ \grave{s} & Z \end{pmatrix} \quad \text{and} \quad \begin{pmatrix} \acute{r} \\ W \end{pmatrix}.$$

If commodities x and y are to be priced at full costs with a uniform mark-up, the prices p and q are defined by

$$\acute{P} = [0, \; p, \; q] = \frac{-1}{\tilde{\phi}_*} \cdot [0, \; \check{e}_x, \; \check{e}_y]$$

$$= \frac{-1}{\tilde{\phi}} [0, \; f, \; g] \cdot (\grave{0}, \; \ulcorner Z^{-1} \grave{W})$$

$$= \frac{-1}{\tilde{\phi}} \begin{pmatrix} 0 & \acute{b} \\ \grave{0} & \tilde{B} \end{pmatrix} \tag{17.15}$$

or, more concisely,

$$\acute{P} = \frac{1}{\tilde{\phi}_*} \cdot \acute{F} \ulcorner B^+$$

where $\ulcorner B^+$ has been named by analogy with (7.6) without commodity-inputs and is identical with the 3 x 3 matrix $(0, \ulcorner Z^{-1}\bar{W})$.

The 'reflexive' transformation compounded of upstream and downstream transformations in sequence is then the result of (17.8) and (17.15); i.e.,

$$\acute{F} = \acute{P}\ulcorner M^+ = \frac{1}{\tilde{\phi}_*} \cdot \acute{F}\ulcorner B^+ \ulcorner M^+ \equiv \frac{1}{\tilde{\phi}_*} \cdot \acute{F}\ulcorner F^+ \tag{17.16}$$

thus defining eigenprices and eigenyield as the latent vector and value of the matrix

$$\ulcorner F^+ \equiv \ulcorner B^+ \ulcorner M^+ \equiv (0, \; \ulcorner Z^{-1}\bar{W})(0, \; \ulcorner X^{-1}\bar{Y}). \tag{17.17}$$

The two separate transformations combined in the reflexive mapping of (17.17) are not altogether easy to interpret in economic terms, but a special effort to do so at this juncture may yield dividends in terms of intuitive understanding: taking the upstream transformation (17.8) first, we note that the matrix $\ulcorner M^+$ contains as its non-zero partition the product $\ulcorner X^{-1}\bar{Y}$, whose elements are first- and second-order derivatives of the capacity constraint $t(x, y; u, v) = b$, as may be seen from (17.1) and (17.4). If the constrained value of $t(= b)$ is regarded as the 'capacity' with which the productive system has to operate, the derivatives t_x and t_y can be interpreted as the marginal 'capacity costs' of the two commodities, while the second-order derivatives t_{xu}, t_{yv}, etc. measure the effectiveness of extra units of the factors in reducing these costs, i.e. the factors' 'capacity-cost saving' or 'capacity-equivalents'.

Further, if we denote the elements of $\ulcorner X^{-1}Y$ by λ_u^+, λ_v^+, x_u^+, etc.

and pre-multiply that matrix by $\ulcorner X$, we find that the product sums that represent the total differentials (with respect to factor inputs) are equated to the factors' capacity-cost savings as recorded in the resultant matrix Y; i.e.,

$$\begin{aligned} \frac{dt}{du} &= t_x x_u^+ + t_y y_u^+ = t_u \\ \frac{dt_x}{du} &= t_x \lambda_u^+ + t_{xx} x_u^+ + t_{xy} y_u^+ = t_{xu} \\ \frac{dt_y}{du} &= t_y \lambda_u^+ + t_{yx} x_u^+ + t_{yy} y_u^+ = t_{yu}. \end{aligned} \tag{17.18}$$

The second two equations make it clear that x_u^+ and y_u^+ are the extra productivities of the factor u required (in conjunction with the λ-productivity λ_u^+) to save the entire capacity costs of the commodities, in fact to reduce all marginal capacity costs to zero, thus 'releasing' the system completely from the capacity constraint to which it was originally subject. We may therefore interpret x_u^+ and y_u^+ as the 'release-productivities' of factor u, and *mutatis mutandis* for factor v. In accordance with this the upstream transformation, (17.18) resolves into:

$$\begin{aligned} [0,\ f,\ g] &= [0,\ p,\ q](0,\ \ulcorner X^{-1}Y) \\ &= [0, p, q]\begin{pmatrix} 0 & \lambda_u^+ & \lambda_v^+ \\ 0 & x_u^+ & x_v^+ \\ 0 & y_u^+ & y_v^+ \end{pmatrix} = \acute{P}\ulcorner M^+ \end{aligned} \tag{17.19}$$

or

$$f = px_u^+ + qy_u^+ \quad \text{and} \quad g = px_v^+ + qy_v^+.$$

Thus, the transformation has the effect of equating the factor-rentals with the commodity-values of the factors' 'release-productivities', an interpretation sufficiently close to that which we have given the (Leontief-type) factor- 'norms' to give us confidence that we are still talking about the same thing, albeit generalized to the nonlinear case.

The downstream transformation (17.15) involves the matrix $(\dot{0},\ \ulcorner Z^{-1}W)$, which can be interpreted as a conspectus of marginal costs:

$$\begin{pmatrix} 0 & \lambda_x^+ & \lambda_y^+ \\ 0 & u_x^+ & u_y^+ \\ 0 & v_x^+ & v_y^+ \end{pmatrix} \equiv \ulcorner\! B^+.$$

Pre-multiplying this matrix by $\ulcorner\! Z$ (defined in connection with (17.13)) we obtain the total differentials of the 'capacity' t with respect to commodity-output x, which are thus equated to the elements of W:

$$\frac{\mathrm{d}t}{\mathrm{d}x} = t_u u_x^+ + t_v v_x^+ = t_x$$

$$\frac{\mathrm{d}t_u}{\mathrm{d}x} = t_u \lambda_x^+ + t_{uu} u_x^+ + t_{uv} v_x^+ = t_{ux} \qquad (17.20)$$

$$\frac{\mathrm{d}t_v}{\mathrm{d}x} = t_v \lambda_x^+ + t_{vu} u_x^+ + t_{vv} v_x^+ = t_{vx}.$$

Given that t_u and t_v are the 'capacity-products' of the two factors, and t_{ux} and t_{vx} the extra factor endowments needed to furnish the additions to these products per unit of commodity x, i.e. the 'replacements' for extra capacity required in terms of factor endowments, we see from the last two equations above that u_x^+ and v_x^+ measure the extra factors required to 'release' the system from its capacity constraint. They could thus be described as the 'release-costs' of x, and *mutatis mutandis* for y (u_y^+ and v_y^+). Accordingly, the downstream transformation (17.15) could be written

$$[0,\ p,\ q] = \frac{1}{\tilde{\phi}_*} \cdot [0,\ f,\ g] \begin{pmatrix} 0 & \lambda_x^+ & \lambda_y^+ \\ 0 & u_x^+ & u_y^+ \\ 0 & v_x^+ & v_y^+ \end{pmatrix}$$

$$= \frac{1}{\tilde{\phi}_*} \cdot \acute{F} \ulcorner\! B^+ \qquad (17.21)$$

or

$$p = \frac{1}{\tilde{\phi}_*} \cdot (f u_x^+ + g v_x^+) \quad \text{and} \quad q = \frac{1}{\tilde{\phi}_*} \cdot (f u_y^+ + g v_y^+).$$

Clearly, this transformation prices the two commodities as the marked-up 'release-costs' in terms of the factor-rentals.

With factor-rentals equal to release-productivities based on commodity-prices, and the latter equal to release-costs in terms of factor-rentals, the way is once again open to a price and rental system that is mutually consistent in the sense of the principle of reciprocal marginality. This is the generalized system of eigenprices defined as the latent vector of the matrix-product $\ulcorner F^{+}$, introduced in (17.16) as

$$\ulcorner F^{+} \equiv \begin{pmatrix} 0 & \lambda_x^{+} & \lambda_y^{+} \\ 0 & u_x^{+} & u_y^{+} \\ 0 & v_x^{+} & v_y^{+} \end{pmatrix} \begin{pmatrix} 0 & \lambda_u^{+} & \lambda_v^{+} \\ 0 & x_u^{+} & x_v^{+} \\ 0 & y_u^{+} & y_v^{+} \end{pmatrix} \equiv \ulcorner B^{+} \cdot \ulcorner M^{+}. \quad (17.22)$$

The nonlinear case thus exactly reproduces the eigenprice definition of the linear case (see (10.4)), except that norm and cost matrices (M and B) cannot now be derived from fixed coefficients or quotas, but must be interpreted as the marginal quantities required to secure release from a nonlinear constraint. It is perfectly possible, by a slight straining of our conceptual apparatus, to look upon the Leontief coefficients in the same light, and in this way to unify the conceptual underpinnings of both linear and nonlinear cases.

To simplify the transformations (17.8) and (17.15) we must eliminate the disturbing 'augmentation' injected by the zero-columns and the remaining border-elements of $\ulcorner H$. When this is done, the transformations of the nonlinear model reduce to

$$\begin{aligned} \acute{f} &\equiv [f, \ g] = [p, \ q]\tilde{M} \equiv \acute{p}\tilde{M} \\ \acute{p} &\equiv [p, \ q] = \frac{1}{\bar{\phi}_*} \cdot [f, \ g]\tilde{B} \equiv \frac{1}{\bar{\phi}_*} \cdot \acute{f}\tilde{B} \end{aligned} \quad (17.23)$$

which accords more closely with the linear (Leontief-type) formulations (8.10).

The nature of $\tilde{M}$ in (17.8) is not far to seek, given that the bordered sub-Hessian $\ulcorner X$ that occurs in that equation has partitions

$$\begin{pmatrix} 0 & \acute{r} \\ \grave{r} & X \end{pmatrix}$$

and therefore inverts into:

$$\ulcorner X^{-1} = \frac{1}{\rho}\left(\begin{array}{c|c} -1 & \acute{r}X^{-1} \\ \hline X^{-1}\grave{r} & \rho X^{-1} - X^{-1}\grave{r}\acute{r}X^{-1} \end{array}\right)$$

$$\text{where } \rho \equiv \acute{r}X^{-1}\grave{r}. \tag{17.24}$$

Post-multiplying this by $\bar{Y}$ whose partitions are $\begin{pmatrix} \acute{s} \\ Y \end{pmatrix}$, we can identify the nonlinear norm-matrix as:

$$\begin{aligned} \tilde{M} &= \frac{1}{\rho}(-X^{-1}\grave{r}\acute{r}X^{-1}Y + X\grave{r}\acute{s} + \rho X^{-1}Y) \\ &= \frac{X^{-1}\grave{r}}{\rho}(\acute{s} - \acute{r}M^{+}) + M^{+}, \text{(where } M^{+} \equiv \acute{r}X^{-1}Y). \end{aligned} \tag{17.25}$$

Further, we can show from the first line of (17.18) and the corresponding v-derivative $\mathrm{d}t/\mathrm{d}v$ that

$$\acute{r}X^{-1}Y = \acute{r}M^{+} = \acute{s} \tag{17.26}$$

and therefore the bracket in the last line of (17.25) vanishes.

Accordingly, the lower right-hand partition of $(0, \ulcorner X^{-1}Y)$ can be identified as

$$\tilde{M} = X^{-1}Y \equiv M^{+} \tag{17.27}$$

with the same meaning as the corresponding partition of $\ulcorner \bar{M}^{+}$, as spelled out in (17.19).

The outcome of analogous operations on $\ulcorner Z^{-1}\bar{W}$ of (17.15) shows that

$$\tilde{B} = Z^{-1}W \equiv B^{+}. \tag{17.28}$$

We can therefore simplify our transformations to

$$\acute{f} = \acute{p}M^{+} \quad \text{and} \quad \acute{p} = \frac{1}{\tilde{\phi}_{*}} \cdot \acute{f}B^{+} \tag{17.29}$$

which establishes that in the nonlinear model our eigenprices and eigenyield are the latent-vector and dominant eigenvalue of the matrix

$$\tilde{F} = \tilde{B}\tilde{M} = Z^{-1}WX^{-1}Y \tag{17.30}$$

all of which are 2×2 partitions of the (unbordered) Hessian of the transformation function $t(x, y; u, v)$.

Note

1 To avoid further forays into recondite mathematics, however essential for full rigour and existence conditions, we assume the second-order conditions to be satisfied throughout.

18

THE PRODUCTION OF COMMODITIES BY MEANS OF COMMODITIES ONLY ('FACTOR-FREE' MODELS)*

The concentration on intrasectoral flows in the production process to the exclusion of primary factors is the preserve of a particular school of theoreticians influenced at several removes by the Marxian schemes of 'production and reproduction' and greatly helped by the new tools forged in Leontief's busy input–output workshop. The device on their banner is 'complementarity' rather than 'substitutability', with the attendant *penchant* for that quasi-engineering approach to economics that has earned them the suspicion, and sometimes revulsion, of their mainstream colleagues. Accused of apostasy from the round table of King Arthur to the square table of King Wassily,[1] they are seen as having abandoned the quest for the Holy Grail in favour of a search for illumination of a radically different sort.

We can, however, throw a bridge to their world by the simple deletion of the third quadrant (W) from our scheme of things (6.1) and its replacement by a direct emanation of the intersectoral flows, giving formal expression to the idea that value-added is dependent not on any importation of inputs from outside the sectoral system, but on a spontaneous secretion of the material inputs themselves – typically proportional to them in size – as if a surplus product had been created by crystalline accretion as a reward for the effort and ingenuity of the labour of combining them.[2]

In effect, this alters our cost-forming equation (7.2), $\acute{c}_r = \acute{c}_r A + \acute{b}_r$, by replacing the second term on the right-hand side by $\alpha \acute{c}_r A$, where α measures the surplus-forming power of the system (or of labour). This substitution defines a rate of surplus, independently of any 'valuation base' (standard factor) r, by the homogeneous equation

$$\acute{c} = \acute{c}A + \alpha\acute{c}A = (1+\alpha)\acute{c}A, \tag{18.1}$$

which may be written more explicitly as

$$\acute{c}\left(\frac{1}{1+\alpha}I - A\right) = \acute{0}. \tag{18.2}$$

This equation shows that our eigencost ratio, as extracted from this particular model, is a simple function of the von Neumann maximal growth-rate α;[3] i.e.,

$$\phi_* = \frac{1}{1+\alpha}, \tag{18.3}$$

while the full-cost vector $\acute{c}$ turns into a particular form of 'diagnostic prices' described by East European analysts as the '*N*-income price system'[4] – a variant of Marxian-type 'channel-prices' which ensures that every sector earns the same rate of value-added (wages + profits + tax-revenue, etc.), or, in other words, that any revenue remaining available after settling expenses on material inputs is distributed (or imputed) in proportion to the material costs borne by the earning sector, regardless of any factor contributions from which it has benefited. If the matrix A is fashioned on Leontief's 'closed model' (i.e. incorporates a row for labour and a column for consumption out of wages), these prices correspond to the classical Marxian 'production prices'.[5]

Our product norms $\grave{k}$, which in this instance are genuine duals of the full-cost values $\acute{c}$, derive from the symmetric notion that the residual outputs left over for final use after the sectors' total input requirements have been met stand in a uniform ratio χ to these requirements, and can therefore be expressed by

$$\grave{k} = Q\grave{k} + \chi Q\grave{k} \quad \text{or} \quad \left(\frac{1}{1+\chi}I - Q\right)\grave{k} = \grave{0}. \tag{18.4}$$

Since Q is 'similar' to A (see (9.1)), its eigenvalue $1/(1+\chi)$ will equal $1/(1+\alpha)$, and χ is therefore equal to the von Neumann growth rate α. The product-norms $\grave{k}$ will then turn out identical with the sectoral contributions to Sraffa's 'representative commodity',[6] defined as the current output-mix measured in such physical units as would make the structure of total inputs $X\grave{i}$ into an exact scale-model of the output structure $\grave{z}$ necessary to supply it, thus allowing the multi-product system to be treated for crucial purposes as if it were a single-sector model measured in terms of the representative commodity.

We cannot of course identify either $\acute{c}$ or $\grave{k}$ with our eigenprices, as the absence of factor-costs deprives the Principle of Reciprocal Marginality of the meaning we have given it in the body of this paper.

Notes

* Leontief case considered only.

1 Reference is here to Professor Wassily Leontif of course.

2 In many instances labour is itself assimilated to the network of intersector flows along with an 'input' column of wage goods consumed by workers, to complete the analogy with production sectors in the 'closed version' of the Leontief analysis.

3 J. V. Neumann, 'A Model of General Economic Equilibrium', *Review of Economic Studies*, vol. 8, 1945/6, pp. 1–9; previously published in German in K. Menger (ed.), *Ergebnisse eines Mathematischen Seminars*, Vienna, 1938. The underlying assumption that every product is involved in every production process ('no whales or wranglers') is spelled out in the accompanying comment to von Neumann's English-language paper by D. G. Champernowne (pp. 10–18).

4 B. Sekerka, O. Kýn, and L. Hejl, 'Price Systems Computable from Input–Output Coefficients', Research Paper no. 15 of the Mathematical Economics Laboratory of the Czechoslovak Academy of Sciences, Prague, 1967, p. 10; also in paper submitted to the Fourth International Conference on Input–Output Techniques, Geneva, 8–10 January 1968.

5 See e.g. András Bródy, 'Three Types of Price Systems', *Economics of Planning*, vol. 5, 1965, pp. 58–66.

6 Piero Sraffa, *The Production of Commodities by Means of Commodities*, Cambridge University Press, 1960, p. 24.

19

'PARTIAL EIGENPRICES – SPECIFIC USES

An obvious extension of eigenprices is the definition of a sub-species generated by narrowing down the final-use contribution (y) that is to serve as the basis for 'norming' to one of the several sub-categories of final use (say α, β, etc.), such as consumption, investment, or defence, which may be singled out as the only one whose benefit is to be reflected in the valuation system. Such 'partial' eigenprices will clearly deviate from the 'total' eigenprices discussed so far, but may be appropriate for special functions or diagnoses relating to an economy. Unfortunately, their exact relation to each other and to total eigenprices is a highly complicated one, not amenable to straightforward formalization in algebraic terms; but a start may be made by offering rigorous definitions of the sub-species in its own right and exploring their possible links with other price-concepts familiar in the literature, though established in different contexts.

It is clear that norming based exclusively on the partial final-use category α, in an economy reduced to two sectors (without loss of generality), will generate product-norms ($\grave{v}^{\alpha}$) defined by equations

$$q_1^1 v_1^{\alpha} + q_1^2 v_2^{\alpha} + p_1 \alpha_1 m_1 = v_1^{\alpha}$$

$$q_2^1 v_1^{\alpha} + q_2^2 v_2^{\alpha} + p_2 \alpha_2 m_2 = v_2^{\alpha}$$

or

$$Q_{v\alpha} + \alpha \hat{m} \grave{p} = \grave{v}^{\alpha} \qquad (19.1)$$

where $\grave{p}$ stands for product-prices (so far arbitrarily imputed), and $\hat{\alpha}$ for the ratios of partial to total final use in each sector, such that $\hat{\alpha} + \hat{\beta} \ldots = 1$. By making this explicit with respect to the product-norms, we obtain

$$\grave{v}_{\alpha} = \overline{Q}^{1}\, \hat{\alpha} \hat{m} \grave{p} \quad or \quad \acute{v}_{\alpha} = \acute{p} \hat{\alpha} \hat{m} \overline{Q}^{1\prime} \qquad (19.2)$$

an equation that corresponds to (8.6) as established for the 'total' case, with $\hat{m}$ replaced by $\hat{\alpha}\hat{m}$. Given these product-norms, the factor-norms $\acute{n}_\alpha$ emerge as

$$\acute{n}_\alpha = \grave{v}_\alpha R' = \acute{p}\hat{\alpha}\hat{m}\overline{Q}^{1\prime}R' = \acute{p}\hat{\alpha}N \tag{19.3}$$

as they did in the 'total' case (see (8.9)), except for the substitution of $\hat{m}$ by $\hat{\alpha}\hat{m}$, and this extablishes the 'upstream' transformation for the partial case. There is no reason why the opposite, 'downstream', transformation should be anything but the familiar costing procedure of (7.6), whether in the total or the partial case, and we therefore have

$$\acute{p}_\alpha = \frac{1}{\phi_\alpha}\acute{f}_\alpha C \tag{19.4}$$

where ϕ_α is now the 'α-eigencost ratio'.

To achieve the complete consistency between product- and factor-prices, which is the distinguishing mark of the genus 'eigenprice', we need only combine equations (19.3) and (19.4), signalling the new-found consistency by substituting $\acute{f}_\alpha$ for the provisional norms $\acute{n}_\alpha$, and $\acute{p}_\alpha$ for the provisional prices $\acute{p}$ in (19.3); i.e.,

$$\acute{f}_\alpha = \acute{p}_\alpha\hat{\alpha}N = \frac{1}{\phi_\alpha}\acute{f}_\alpha C\hat{\alpha}N \equiv \frac{1}{\phi_\alpha}\acute{f}_\alpha F_\alpha. \tag{19.5}$$

The 'α-eigenprices' and 'α-eigencost ratio' are therefore the eigenvector and dominant eigenvalue of the matrix $C\hat{\alpha}N$, while the total eigenprices were similarly related to the matrix $CN(\equiv F)$. The only change is thus the reduction of all norms in the ratio that the selected use-category bears to the total final use of each product.

A particular variant of partial eigenprices, where the norm-base is the portion of final use entering the trade balance, i.e. export net of import, is worthy of special attention. We may call them 'foreign-trade-geared' or 'external' eigenprices, and can define them in accordance with (19.5) by the simple device of replacing α by ϵ:

$$\acute{f}_\epsilon = \frac{1}{\phi_\epsilon}\acute{f}_\epsilon C\hat{\epsilon}N \quad \text{or} \quad \acute{f}_\epsilon(\phi_\epsilon I - C\hat{\epsilon}N) = \acute{0} \tag{19.6}$$

where $\hat{\epsilon}$ is the ratio of net export to the total final use of each sector's product.

The last-quoted formulation enables us to relate external to total eigenprices in the particular case where net exports absorb a *uniform* proportion ϵ of the final use of each product. The diagonal matrix $\hat{\epsilon}$ then changes into the unit matrix multiplied by a scalar (ϵI), and (19.6) can be written

$$\epsilon \acute{f}^*_\epsilon \left(\frac{\phi_\epsilon}{\epsilon} I - F \right) = \acute{0}. \tag{19.7}$$

This is clearly identical with the definition of total eigenprices (10.4), with prices $\acute{f}$ turning into $\epsilon \acute{f}_\epsilon$ and the total eigencost ratio from ϕ_* into ϕ_ϵ / ϵ. In this particular case, therefore, external eigenprices can be shown to be equal to total eigenprices scaled up by the net export ratio, while the external eigencost ratio is correspondingly scaled down. Clearly, such a rescaling makes sense only when applied to eigenprices that have already been scaled or 'standardized' in the first place (see Chapter 12 above), a fact to which we draw attention by starring the relevant symbols in the equations:

$$\acute{f}_e = \frac{1}{\epsilon} \acute{f}_* \quad \text{and} \quad \phi_\epsilon = \epsilon \phi_*. \tag{19.8}$$

The resulting external prices $\acute{f}_e$, however, are no longer 'standardized' themselves, since their internal product with the sectoral value-added elements $\grave{\omega}$ would no longer be equal to the total national income ω_0, as required by standardization (see Chapter 12), but would reach the higher level $(1/\epsilon)\acute{f}_*\grave{\omega}$; i.e., $(1/\epsilon)\omega_0$. In order to achieve proper 'scaling to national income', therefore, the external rentals of (19.8) would themselves need to be scaled down in the proportion ϵ; i.e.,

$$\acute{f}^*_e = \epsilon \acute{f}_e = \acute{f}_*. \tag{19.9}$$

The same is true of the external eigenprices of commodities $\acute{p}_e$, which can be derived from the partial eigenrentals as

$$\acute{p}_e = \frac{1}{\phi_e} \acute{f}_e F_e = \frac{1}{\epsilon \phi_*} \acute{f}_e \epsilon F = \frac{1}{\epsilon \phi_*} \acute{f}_* F = \frac{1}{\epsilon} \acute{p}_*. \tag{19.10}$$

As they stand these would 'overvalue' the GNP ($\acute{p}_* \grave{y}$) by the factor $1/\epsilon$ and must therefore be scaled down by the factor ϵ, in the same way as the external eigenrentals; i.e.,

$$\acute{p}^*_e = \epsilon \acute{p}_e = \acute{p}_*. \tag{19.11}$$

Thus we conclude that, in the particular case of an export ratio (ϵ) applying *uniformly* to all products, external prices remain equal to total eigenprices, and only the eigencost ratio is affected in the proportion ϵ, as shown in (19.8).

20

OECD SHADOW PRICES FOR PROJECT APPRAISAL

These prices, occasionally dubbed 'Little-Mirrlees', in deference to the authors of the relevant OECD manual,[1] have now acquired so much influence that some exploration of their kinship with eigenprices, particularly of the 'external' variety (Chapter 19), seems to be called for. Although the use of foreign trade or 'border' prices, which lies at the basis of the Manual, strongly suggests such a kinship, it will turn out to be a fairly remote and even deceptive one. Nevertheless some attention to it, however summary and impressionistic, will increase our understanding of both the price systems under comparison.

It should be understood from the outset that the purpose of the OECD prices is not the construction of a generalized or self-consistent system, but the provision of relatively simple tools enabling project-appraisers who are not necessarily sophisticated economists to find short cuts to difficult decisions, vastly more sensible and productive of economic benefit than could be achieved by reliance on market prices. In that the Manual brilliantly succeeds, and its success is by no means tarnished by the lack of internal consistency on which we shall have to dwell. After all, consistency is often a very minor virtue, the panoply of the intellectually timid or the fig-leaf of the sexless, and its absence may betoken no more than a healthy contempt for redundant clothing on the part of those who have no such defects to hide.

In the second place, it should be understood that the Manual's reliance on the 'border prices' of foreign trade[2] is in no way intended to make foreign trade or the acquisition of foreign currency into the be-all and end-all of an economy. It merely identifies the most direct and simple indicators of the terms on which an economy can substitute one product for another. In an economy too small to affect world prices by its own demand and supply behaviour (such as the Manual assumes), these terms can most readily be ascertained by consulting the foreign trade prices payable for imports or exports of commodities at the country's borders, without the inconvenience and risk of error involved in complicated input–output calculations. It is then a relatively easy matter to compute price ratios for 'non-traded' goods and factors on this directly ascertainable basis.

In offering a formalization of border prices ($\acute{u}$) in this section, we would not wish to commit the authors of the OECD manual to this particular interpretation of their brainchild. We have, however, based our own applied study of the system (commissioned by one of these authors via the OECD)[3] on this interpretation, and have not been made aware of any protest in this respect.

We start by dividing the economy into a department of, say, three sectors (suffix $o = 1, 2, 3$) producing 'non-tradables' which are neither exported nor imported, and one of the two sectors (suffix $x = 4, 5$) producing 'tradables' whose predominant origin or destination is foreign and whose border prices are π_4 and π_5 respectively. We also distinguish two domestic factors, a and b, whose 'border prices' v_a and v_b are determined by aggregation of tradable border prices, as are those of the non-tradable sectors $\acute{u}_o = (u_1, u_2, u_3)$. Of course, the choice of 3, 2, and 2 for the number of sectors and factors is in substitution for the abstract numbers n_0, n_x, and m for expository purposes only, and implies no departure from generality. The conspectus of intersector flows in such an economy takes the form shown in (20.1).

$$
\begin{array}{l|l|l|l|l}
 & x_1^1 + x_1^2 + x_1^3 & + x_1^4 + x_1^5 & + d_1^a + d_1^b + j_1 & = z_1 \\
\text{Non-tradables} & x_2^1 + x_2^2 + x_2^3 & + x_2^4 + x_2^5 & + d_2^a + d_2^b + j_2 & = z_2 \\
\quad (o) & x_3^1 + x_3^2 + x_3^3 & + x_3^4 + x_3^5 & + d_3^a + d_3^b + j_3 & = z_3 \\
\hline
\text{Tradables} & x_4^1 + x_4^2 + x_4^3 & + x_4^4 + x_4^5 & + d_4^a + d_4^b + j_4 & = z_4 \\
\quad (x) & x_5^1 + x_5^2 + x_5^3 & + x_5^4 + x_5^5 & + d_5^a + d_5^b + j & = z_5 \\
\hline
 & w_a^1 + w_a^2 + w_a^3 & + w_a^4 + w_a^5 & & = w_a \\
\text{Factors} & w_b^1 + w_b^2 + w_b^3 & + w_b^4 + w_b^5 & & = w_b
\end{array}
\qquad (20.1)
$$

or, in matrix terms,

Non-tradables	$X_o^o \grave{i}$	$+ X_o^x \grave{i}$	$+ \grave{d}_o^a + d_o^b + \grave{j}_o = \grave{z}_o$
Tradables	$X_x^o \grave{i}$	$+ X_x^x \grave{i}$	$+ \grave{d}_x^a + \grave{d}_x^b + \grave{j}_x = \grave{z}_x$
Factors	$W^o \grave{i}$	$+ W^x \grave{i}$	$= \grave{w}$

where previously used symbols retain their meaning, while $(\grave{d}^a, \grave{d}^b) \equiv D$ stand for the products bought by the two factors out of their rewards for current productive services, and $\grave{j}$ represent final uses not held to be in the line of factor rewards. It goes almost without saying that the D-variables will in practice be very difficult to ascertain, but the crucial column listing the wage-goods consumed by 'labour' should be amenable to estimation from workers' family budget data, so that the method of the Manual is quite easily applicable to the one main (and possibly only) factor of production in respect of which the Manual recommends its special procedure. In what follows, however, we shall assume, for the sake of completeness and consistency, that the procedure is, conceptually at least, applicable to all the factors distinguished in (20.1), thereby departing from the detailed simplifications of the Manual.

With the border prices of tradables (π_x) culled from foreign trade statistics and adjusted for trade and transport costs to and from the border, the 'border-price contents'[4] of non-tradables ($\acute{u}_o$) and of factors ($\acute{v}$) are implicitly defined by the Manual or its commentators[5] as follows

$$\begin{aligned} \acute{u}_o X_o^o + \acute{\pi} X_x^o + \acute{v} W^o &= \acute{u}_o \hat{z}_o \\ \acute{u}_o D_o + \acute{\pi} D_x &= \acute{v} \hat{w}. \end{aligned} \tag{20.2}$$

Post-multiplying the first of these equations by $\hat{z}_o^{-1}$ and the second by $\hat{w}^{-1}$, we obtain the usual restatement of the scheme in terms of input-coefficients:

$$\begin{aligned} \acute{u}_o A_o^o + \acute{\pi} A_x^o + \acute{v} B^o &= \acute{u}_o \\ \acute{u}_o E_o + \acute{\pi} E_x &= \acute{v} \end{aligned} \tag{20.3}$$

where the only new symbols are E, standing for factor consumption per unit factor-use ($\equiv D w^{-1}$).

The reader will easily recognize in the first equation of (20.3) an exact replica of our costing procedure (7.2), this time restricted to non-tradables, with border-prices tradables entering into the cost-structure on a par with factors, and factors themselves being priced at $\acute{v}$, a set of rentals defined by the second equation.

It should be noted here that in defining the shadow prices of tradables the Manual departs from the cost-aggregation principle applied to the case of non-tradables (i.e., $\acute{u}_x$ is not defined by $\acute{u}_x X_o^x + \acute{\pi} X_x^x + \acute{v} W^x = \acute{u}_x \hat{z}_x$), but sets them equal to directly observable 'border prices' culled from foreign trade statistics (i.e, $\acute{u}_x = \acute{\pi}$). In consequence, there is nothing to ensure that the prices of domestically produced tradables are in any way related to domestic costs, even to those calculable in terms of border-price-related non-tradable or factor-prices. The equality of prices with average (or marginal) costs is thus clearly violated in the 'tradables' domain, and the principle of price determination for particular products becomes dependent on the domain to which they have been allocated. Given that the Manual gives only impressionistic guidance on the criteria for this allocation ('predominant' origin or destination of the product), the structure of the shadow prices emerging could easily become dependent on the 'free-hand' judgement of the project-appraiser or on his assiduity in combing foreign trade statistics for usable 'border prices' to help in the exercise.[6]

Moreover, as the second equations of (20.2) and (20.3) show, the factor-prices are equated to the 'border-price contents' of the purchases made by factor-owners out of their current incomes, and are thus aimed to reflect only the economic *costs* of factor utilization without regard to the productivities of the factors in terms of final goods. There is no reference to the 'use' component of value implicit in the 'norms' that enter into eigenprices; and this, in conjunction with the almost exclusive attention paid to labour among the factors of production, brings the recommendations of the Manual much more into line with the Marxian 'cost-fetishist' and 'factor-monomaniac' position than is widely appreciated.

Nevertheless, the Manual injects an element of 'valuation by use' through a number of adjustments recommended for the calculation of shadow-wages, which allow for the fact that some of the wages paid by a project reflect a raising of consumption levels in line with what is socially desirable in low-income countries and therefore do not constitute a 'cost' to the economy in the true sense of the term. These adjustments, with their hint at an unspecified, but implicitly assumed, social welfare function, could with every justification be cited in the Manual's defence against the accusation of cost-fetishism.

To find explicit expressions for the border prices of all products and factors we need only solve equations (20.3) and substitute in the first the value of $\acute{v}$ found from the second, thus obtaining

$$\acute{u}_o(A_o^o + E_oB^o) + \acute{\pi}(A_x + E_xB^o) = \acute{u}_o. \tag{20.4}$$

By writing G_o and G_x for the two bracketed expressions, we obtain finally:

$$\acute{u}_o = \acute{\pi}G_x(I - G_o)^{-1} \tag{20.5}$$

where

$$G_o \equiv A_o^o + E_oB^o$$

and

$$G_x \equiv A_x^o + E_xB^o. \tag{20.6}$$

The last two statements will enable us to specify the steps necessary to convert 'border prices' into total eigenprices as defined in (10.4).

1 The absorption of tradables by sectors producing non-tradables must be subsumed under factor-inputs W^o (possibly as part of the absorption of 'complementary imports'). This dispenses with the 'domain' suffixes x and o, and eliminates the matrix X_x^o, thus converting the first equation of (20.3) into

$$\acute{u}A + \acute{v}B = \acute{u} \tag{20.7}$$

and the second into

$$\acute{u}E = \acute{v}. \tag{20.8}$$

The solution of the two converted equations ($EB\overline{A}^{\rceil}$), when scaled up to allow for uniform profit, is therefore

$$\acute{u} = \frac{1}{\phi}\,uEB\overline{A}^{\rceil} = \frac{1}{\phi}\,uEC \tag{20.9}$$

thus making the prices $\acute{u}$ into an eigenvector of the matrix EC (corresponding to the dominant ϕ).

2 The matrix E must be assumed to have the 'dyadic' form $\grave{e}\acute{v}$, embodying the assumption that the common human biology of all factor-owners forces each of them to consume a subsistence-basket of uniform composition $\grave{e}$ (per unit output), or at least that only the consumption of such baskets can properly be regarded as their factor-reward, while any deviation from it is the result of 'discretionary' expenditure unrelated to *necessary* rewards for productive services. The difference between the total rewards paid out to various factors (i.e. between the columns of E) is therefore solely one of scale, as determined by the difference between their costs (given by the vector $\acute{v}$).

3 The proper valuation of the final uses of all commodities (per unit output) must be unity ($\acute{u}\grave{y} = 1$), and that of the subsistence-basket $\grave{e}$ (per unit output), that proportion of the national income which is mortgaged to the necessary reward of factors; i.e.,

$$\acute{u}\grave{e} = \phi. \tag{20.10}$$

The assumptions of this and the preceding note lead to the equation

$$\acute{u} = \frac{1}{\phi}\,\acute{u}\grave{e}\acute{v}c = \acute{v}C \tag{20.11}$$

thus replacing the costing equation (7.5).

4 Finally, when replacing costs by full-cost prices, and requiring product-prices and factor-rentals to be mutually consistent (signalled by the replacement of $\acute{u}$ and $\acute{v}$ by $\acute{p}$ and $\acute{f}$), we arrive at the two eigenprice-generating transformations:

$$\acute{p} = \frac{1}{\phi}\,\acute{f}C \quad \text{and} \quad \acute{f} = \acute{p}N \tag{20.12}$$

as per (10.1), which uniquely determine the previously arbitrary factor-rentals $\acute{v}$ by equating them to the eigenvector of $CN (\equiv F)$ corresponding to the dominant ϕ_*.

The four steps outlined above serve to establish a remote but discernible kinship between eigenprices and OECD border price valuations, differentiating the latter from the former in the main by virtue of their separate treatment of tradable products as original factor-inputs subject to special pricing rules, and by the 'cost-fetishist' valuation of other factors independently of use or productivity considerations. They also make it clear that the kinship, however remote it may be, is as much with 'total' eigenprices as with partial, 'external' eigenprices, which, in spite of their orientation towards foreign trade, are neither in practice nor in theory any nearer OECD prices than eigenprices in their most general definition.

Notes

1 Ian M. D. Little and James A. Mirrlees, *Manual of Industrial Project Analysis in Developing Countries*. vol. II, *Social Cost Benefit Analysis*, Development Centre of the Organization for Economic Co-operation and Development, Paris, 1969; henceforth referred to as 'the Manual'.

2 The term 'border prices' is not used in the Manual itself, which prefers a variety of less descriptive expressions like 'shadow-prices' or 'accounting prices', but it has been widely adopted by subsequent commentators as a handy and fairly accurate label.

3 Francis Seton, *Shadow Wages in Chile*, OECD, Paris, 1972, and 'Shadow Wages in Chile', in R. S. Eckaus and P. N. Rosenstein-Rodan (eds.), *Analysis of Development Problems*, North-Holland Publishing Company, Amsterdam 1973.

4 The expression 'border-price content' seems more appropriate than 'border prices' or 'derived border prices' when applied to non-tradables or factors.

5 See in particular Seton, *Shadow Wages in the Chilean Economy*, Eckaus and Rosenstein-Rodan, *Analysis of Development Problems*, pp. 49–119.

6 This search will often be complicated or frustrated by disparities in the definition or breakdown of productive sectors between input–output data and foreign trade statistics (e.g. tariff data), the latter being typically available only in such detailed breakdowns (by quality, weight, chemical composition, etc.) as to require painstaking and uncertain aggregation procedures before even a semblance of harmonization can be achieved.

21
'PARTIAL' EIGENPRICES – SPECIFIC FACTORS

The cost-analogue of restricting the eigenprice base to specific final *uses* is clearly a similar restriction in respect of the *factors* or the types of their renumeration that are to be accounted as costs.

This has particular relevance when important parts of government revenue are raised by drawing on factor incomes *after* they have accrued and entered input–output statistics, i.e. by imposing 'direct' taxes or levies on wages, profits, rental incomes, etc. If the 'true' rewards of factors are to be measured in such cases, the pre-tax factor input matrix W in scheme (6.1) and the corresponding matrices of coefficients (B) and costs (C) must in each sector be reduced in a proportion a equal to the ratio of pre-tax to post-tax income ($= 1 - t$, where t is the average rate of direct taxation).

Allowing discrimination in tax rates between production sectors, but not factors, the downstream transformation (7.6) would be:

$$\acute{p}_a = \frac{1}{\phi_a} \acute{f}_a \hat{a} C \tag{21.1}$$

where $\hat{a}$ is the diagonal matrix of post-tax to pre-tax value-added in the various sectors, $\acute{p}_a$ and $\acute{f}_a$ the product- and factor-prices generated by this tax regime, and ϕ_a the post-tax eigenratio yet to be computed.

With the upstream transformation $\acute{f} = \acute{p}N$ unaltered except for the suffixes a, the partial eigenrentals $\acute{f}_a$ are the solutions of

$$\acute{f}_a = \frac{1}{\phi_a} \acute{f}_a \hat{a} F \quad \text{or} \quad \acute{f}_a(\phi_a I - \hat{a}F) = \acute{0}. \tag{21.2}$$

ϕ_a and $\acute{f}_a$ are thus the eigenvalue and eigenvector of the matrix $\hat{a}F$, instead of those of F, which would generate the *total* eigenvalues ϕ and $\acute{f}$.

We can compare the two systems most clearly (but not explicitly) by juxtaposing the two characteristic equations:

$$\text{post-tax:} \quad \acute{f}_a \hat{a}(\phi_a \hat{a}^{-1} - F) = \acute{0}$$

$$\text{pre-tax:} \quad \acute{f}(\phi_* I - F) = \acute{0}. \tag{21.3}$$

If we drive simplification to the point where direct tax rates are uniform as between sectors, thus reducing the matrix $\hat{a}$ to aI (where a is a scalar), we can perform an explicit comparison by rewriting the post-tax equation as

$$a\acute{f}_a \left(\frac{\phi_a}{a} I - F \right) = \acute{0}. \tag{21.4}$$

This makes it clear that the relationship between the post- and pre-tax values in such a case would be

$$\acute{f}_a = \acute{f}^*/a \quad \text{and} \quad \phi_a = a\phi_*. \tag{21.5}$$

In other words, the eigenrentals are scaled up, and the eigencost ratio scaled down, in proportion to post- and pre-tax ratio $a(= 1 - t$, where t is the average tax rate), assuming always that prices and rentals are scaled or 'standardized' to start with. If, however, the resulting partial eigenrentals $\acute{f}_a$ are themselves to be standardized, they must again be scaled down in the ratio a, thus remaining equal to the standardized total eigenprices ($\acute{f}_a^* = \acute{f}^*$). Just as in the case of external eigenprices (19.9), therefore, the restriction of value-forming factors to a *uniform* proportion of total value-added in each sector will leave the standardized total eigenprices unaffected, and will merely scale down the eigencost ratio in the same proportion (a). A change in eigenprices will be brought about only if the base-factor varies as a proportion of total value-added from sector to sector.

22
MARXIAN LABOUR VALUES

In an extreme case we might eliminate all factors other than labour and thus approximate the Marxian labour-values, although for a *complete* assimilation to these concepts we would need to add a number of further steps. In particular, we would need to dispense with the use-norming of factors and restrict ourselves to a downstream transformation like (21.1) with the diagonal $\hat{a}$ interpreted as the ratio of wages to total value-added, even though this would leave the factor-rentals $\acute{f}_a$ still to be determined.

For this determination the Marxian system allows us two options.

1 We could accept the verdict of the market (or of the price bureau in centrally planned economics) and value the factors in current money prices as recorded in the original input–output scheme, thus equating $\acute{f}_a$ with the first row of the unit-matrix $\acute{i}_1$, where the first element is unity and all others zero. With $\hat{a}$ measuring wage to value-added ratios this would amount to accepting actual wage payments as the proper measure of labour contributions per unit output, i.e., $\acute{a} = w\acute{i}_1$ (where w is the average money wage per hour), while disqualifying all other factor contributions by setting ϕ_a equal to 1. This converts our downstream transformation to

$$\acute{\lambda}_i = w\acute{i}_1 C = w\acute{i}_1 B\overline{A}^{\rceil} = \acute{b}_1\overline{A}^{\rceil} = \acute{b}_1\overline{A}^{\rceil} \qquad (22.1)$$

where w is set equal to 1 in line with the Marxian practice of measuring labour contributions in terms of labour-hours themselves, and $\acute{b}_1$ is the first row of the factor-input coefficient matrix B, a definition that replicates the previously established formula (7.3) for the case where $\acute{b}_r = \acute{b}_1$ and refers to the factor-inputs of labour. This is the straightforward, *first* definition of the Marxian labour-values, which I have elsewhere called the definition *by imputation* ($\acute{\lambda}_i$).[1]

2 The second option would base itself on an alternative definition '*by alienation*' ($\acute{\lambda}_a$), also due to Marx. Here we drive cost-fetishism to the ultimate extreme by valuing labour contributions as the cost of 'labour-power' (in terms of consumption out of wages) marked up by a 'rate of exploitation' (ψ), uniformly applied to all product costings. This assumes that, in addition to the *material* input coefficients A, we also know the consumption coefficient matrix H whose n columns are the consumption purchases (out of wages) of workers engaged in the various production sectors per unit output, so that the total prime-cost inputs in real terms are $G(\equiv A + H)$ products per unit output, and the 'global' (direct and indirect) prime costs are the columns of the 'synthesized' matrix $G\overline{A}^{\rceil}$. To this must be added in each sector the column of 'exploited' (unpaid) labour inputs ψH, thus defining the Marxian values as

$$\acute{\lambda}_a = \acute{\lambda}_a(G\overline{A}^{\rceil} + \psi H\overline{A}^{\rceil}) = \acute{\lambda}_a A\overline{A}^{\rceil} + \acute{\lambda}_a H\overline{A}^{\rceil} + \psi\acute{\lambda}_a H\overline{A}^{\rceil}. \quad (22.2)$$

Those familiar with the Marxian theory will recognize on the extreme right-hand side the familiar analysis of value into 'constant' capital, 'variable' capital, and the 'surplus' ($c + v + s$), all measured in terms of labour value themselves, and the constant ψ as the Marxian 'rate of exploitation'.

The last equation enables us to define the Marxian values in a manner that parallels the definition of eigenprices; i.e.,

$$\acute{\lambda}_a \left(\frac{1}{1+\psi} I - H\overline{A}^{\rceil} \right) = \acute{0} \quad (22.3)$$

where the eigenvalue $1/(1 + \psi)$ is obviously akin to the eigencost ratio ϕ_*, but the matrix furnishing that eigenvalue (and the corresponding eigenvector $\acute{v}_a$) is the matrix of direct and indirect ('synthesized') consumption coefficients of labour $H\overline{A}^{\rceil}$ instead of the norm-cost matrix $P(= NC)$ which furnishes eigencost and eigenprices (ϕ and $\acute{p}$).

It is possible to show that, given certain assumptions implicit in the Marxian system, the two definitions of value ($\acute{\lambda}_i$ and $\acute{\lambda}_a$ in (22.1) and (22.3)) are equivalent. The crucial assumptions derive from the doctrine that under capitalism the real wage is never more than a subsistence ration. This implies

1 that all households consume the same product-mix per unit output, say $\grave{h}$, and the columns of the consumption-input matrix H will

only differ by constant factors measuring the amount of labour used per unit output in the various production sectors; i.e.,

$$H = \grave{h}\acute{l}; \tag{22.4}$$

2 that households need to consume all their wages and cannot save (in terms of value); that is, that the value of the uniform consumption-basket $\grave{h}$ is equal to the portion of the total labour contribution[1] that is paid for. In other words,

$$\acute{\lambda}_a\grave{h} = \frac{1}{1+\psi} \equiv \text{the Marxian cost ratio } \phi_m. \tag{22.5}$$

Given the two implications (22.4) and (22.5), we can write the definition *by alienation* (22.3) as

$$\acute{\lambda}_a\left(\frac{1}{1+\psi}I - \grave{h}\acute{l}A\right) = \frac{1}{1+\psi}\acute{\lambda}_a - \acute{\lambda}_a\grave{h}\acute{\lambda}_i = \frac{1}{1+\psi}(\acute{\lambda}_a - \acute{\lambda}_i) = 0. \tag{22.6}$$

In other words, $\acute{\lambda}_a = \acute{\lambda}_i \equiv \acute{\lambda}$, and the equivalence of the two Marxian definition is proved.

A straightforward comparison of eigenprices $\acute{p}$ and Marxian labour-values $\acute{\lambda}$ would thus take the form

$$\begin{aligned} \acute{p}(\phi I - NC) &= \acute{0} \\ \acute{\lambda}\left(\frac{1}{1+\psi}I - H\overline{A}^{\rceil}\right) &= \acute{0}. \end{aligned} \tag{22.7}$$

It is clear, therefore that eigenprices would turn into labour-values if the household consumption of workers per unit output H could be accepted as the true 'use-norms' of factors (NB), and the global (direct and indirect) absorption of material inputs ($\overline{A}^{\rceil}$) as the true 'costs' of commodities (C). In this case the eigencost ratio would turn into the ratio in which wage payments (i.e. 'unexploited' labour) stood to total value-added (i.e. the total contribution of labour), i.e. $\phi = 1/(1+\psi)$.

Eigenprices must, however, deviate from labour-values to the extent that the issue is not prejudged in this way, and both norms and costs are derived from the transformation (or production) functions under which the economy actually operates.

A similar reduction of the eigenprice system, this time focusing on the eigencost ratio, will serve to make explicit its relationship to the Marxian rate of exploitation (ψ) and the latter's derivative cost ratio

ϕ_m, i.e. the proportion of 'paid' to total (paid and unpaid) labour. In line with the single-factor model of the Marxian scheme, we must set

$$W = \acute{w}_1 ; B = W\hat{z}^{-1} = \acute{b}_1 ; \hat{w} = w_1 = L \text{ (total labour)} \qquad (22.8)$$

and

$$R = \hat{w}^{-1}W = \acute{w}_1/L = \acute{r}_1 . \qquad (22.9)$$

The cost matrix C is thereby reduced to the row-vector of labour-values:

$$C = B\overline{A}\rceil = \acute{b}_1\overline{A}\rceil = \acute{\lambda} \qquad (22.10)$$

and the norm-matrix, in line with (9.3), to the column-vector of final products valued in eigenprices per unit labour in use; i.e.,

$$N = \hat{y}C'w^{-1} = \frac{1}{L}\,\hat{y}\grave{\lambda} = \grave{y}_\lambda/L . \qquad (22.11)$$

Since $L(= \acute{b}_1\grave{z})$ is by virtue of (6.7) equal to $\acute{b}_1\overline{A}\rceil\grave{y}$ and therefore equals $\acute{\lambda}\grave{y}$ or Σy_λ, the last expression in (22.11) represents the structure of final demand in terms of eigenprices, an obvious weighting system for any set of commodity-prices $\acute{p}$ to be transformed into the single factor-norm (or revenue productivity) of labour f_1 (see (8.10)). It follows from the last two equations that the cost-norm matrix $F(= CN)$ whose dominant furnishes the eigencost ratio reduces to a scalar (which is its own dominant); i.e.,

$$\phi_* = \text{dom.}\, CN = \acute{\lambda}\grave{y}_\lambda/L = \bar{\lambda} . \qquad (22.12)$$

The eigencost ratio thus reduces to a weighted mean or average of the labour values with the eigenpriced final demands serving as weights.

To contrast this with the Marxian cost ratio, we need only remind ourselves of the Marxian assumption (22.5):

$$\phi_m = \acute{\lambda}\grave{h},$$

a weighted sum of the same labour-values that figure in the single-factor eigencost ratio (22.12), but with weights now reduced from the *total* final supply of each sector per unit GNP to the supply for wage-financed consumption per unit output of each sector and the weights expressed in currently priced instead of labour-valued supplies.

We may therefore identify the Marxian value system as a special subspecies of eigenprices reduced to 'partial' coverage on both the factor- and the final-use side (Chapters 19 and 21), in which, moreover, the norming of the single factor is based on 'untransformed' weighting of commodity-prices and which to that extent falls short of complete consistency.

Notes

1 Francis Seton, 'The Question of Ideological Obstacles to Rational Price Setting in Communist Countries', in Alan Abouchar (ed.), *The Socialist Price Mechanism*, Duke University Press, Durham, NC, 1977, pp. 10–39.

23

EIGENPRICES – A SUMMARY OF BASIC CHARACTERISTICS

The many ramifications and parallels of eigenprices we have passed in review may have confused and exhausted the reader to the point where the essential meaning and purport of this unfamiliar price concept have been lost. It may be helpful, therefore, to offer a short and non-rigorous recapitulation at this point.

It seems best to start with the key concept of the 'eigencost ratio' ϕ, the eigenvalue of a defined matrix, from which the whole system takes its name.

Imagine a government forced to observe two principles in its revenue-raising (possibly imposed by some legally enthroned supra-national watchdog or legislative commission):

1. It is debarred from enforcing unilateral transfers (i.e. direct taxes) out of incomes once they have accrued in return for factor services rendered, as this is regarded as spoliation. It can therefore get its (unearned) revenue only by 'indirect' (price-boosting) taxation.
2. Its taxes must not discriminate against any factor or branch of production.

The upshot of this would be a value-added tax (VAT) levied at a uniform rate from all sectors of production. The 'eigenyield' $\sigma_*(=1/\phi_* - 1)$ is then the VAT rate the government would be able to impose if all factors earned their 'due' income (= marginal revenue productivity) without monopoly rents or other economically unjustified perks obtained by extortion or deceit, and if all products were sold at factor cost *plus* the VAT (= uniformly marked-up marginal cost). We believe we have shown that this VAT rate is computable and a unique function[1] of the coefficients and quotas of the 'Leontief technology'.[2]

The corresponding factor-rentals and prices form the system of 'eigenprices' – equally unique (up to a multiplicative constant) and specific to the economy under review.

We believe that these prices can be used for the computation of internal ratios of a structural or cost–benefit kind, and can enable unbiased comparisons of these to be made across time, space, and economic systems. The index-number problem is thereby avoided for *ratio* comparisons, though not for comparisons of *absolutes*; the latter must still await the formulation of internationally valid eigenprice systems which, though possibly definable on similar principles, are left outside the scope of this book as unfinished business.

For the computation of ϕ_* the direct taxes actually imposed ought to be obtained from factor-incomes before the calculation begins. If they cannot be (for lack of statistics), the ϕ-measure and corresponding eigenyield σ are vitiated. If they can be, these measures are clearly affected by arbitrary tax rates as well as technological imperatives, but are still meaningful if the tax rates are imposed by a democratically elected government and therefore represent what the factor-owners are collectively prepared to put up with. Even where tax rates are undemocratically enforced, however, they retain an economic meaning as measures of what the government is able to 'get out' of the factors, however unwilling they may be. Our σ is therefore best regarded not as a measure of efficiency *per se*, but as the combined effect of efficiency and self-abnegation (voluntary or enforced) which is perhaps best captured by the notion of 'cost effectiveness'. Inefficient military dictatorship might achieve lower ϕ_* (higher σ_*) than efficient consumer societies under the sway of free collective bargaining. Just as growth in productivity can fail to benefit living standards owing to faster population growth, so superiority in technology and the state of the arts might fail to yield greater 'cost effectiveness' owing to parallel leads in real wages, profit-taking, and consumerism.

We conclude that the ϕ_*-measure must be treated with circumspection, but that it does capture a characteristic of the economy that is worth watching and comparing between different times, countries, and economic systems.

Notes

1 But for problems relating to the existence and uniqueness of an economically meaningful dominant eigenroot of the relevant 'valuation matrices' F and P (10.4).

2 Including also factor-input coefficients valued at the remuneration exacted or accepted by the factor-owners concerned.

24
EIGENPRICES – POSSIBLE USES

24a International and intertemporal comparison

This aspect of the matter has been fully explored in previous chapters and, indeed, provided the first impetus for the designing and construction of eigenprices. It is the comparison of *ratios* that is at issue, to be sure, and not a comparison of aggregates or absolute levels; but in this restricted sphere at least it may fairly be claimed that eigenprices are unbiased and relevant standards of comparison. They measure economic flows in terms of a yardstick reflecting each economy's own implicit view of the relative urgency of wants and scarcity of resources – the view that has motivated its economy to produce the observed network of physical flows in what was presumably a search for the greatest possible satisfaction of wants, whether individual or collective, in the face of existing constraints.

In Part III we shall test the general plausibility of the results obtainable from using eigenprices in this way.

24b Diagnostic use

Standardized eigenprices below unity reflect an overvaluation of the relevant sectoral products in terms of the operative price system, and therefore pinpoint the existence of monopoly elements or other conditions enhancing the capacity of the sectoral producers to exact higher rewards from their buyers than their rationally measured contributions to the economy justify. The same is true of factor-owners whose eigenrentals are below unity. Unless distributional considerations outweigh purely economic criteria, therefore, these deviations present a prima facie case for scrutinizing institutional arrangements, customs, or tax-subsidy regimes with a view to reducing such excessive rewards in the interests of allocational efficiency. The signal that this was on the way to being achieved would be the gradual reduction of the offending prices towards the level of the corresponding eigenprices. To the extent that this would not automatically bring about the raising in the price of *under*valued commodities or factors (those with eigenprices *above* unity), opposite measures would need to be undertaken to counteract the non-economic disabilities under which these sectors (or factors) were operating.

In countries where rentals and prices are centrally controlled, of course, the adjustment in the direction of eigenprices could be undertaken by altering operative prices directly by *fiat*. However, if this were not accompanied by institutional measures to remove the concentrations of 'extra-economic' power or disadvantage, it would result in putatively undesired changes in the final physical flows produced. In either case, therefore, the response to deviations from eigenprices would need to contain a strong element of institutional, legal, or fiscal readjustment. The mere change of operative prices to bring them into line with eigenprices would not be enough, unless such a movement was the result of deeper changes in the necessary direction.

It can therefore be said that eigenprices provide the means for a diagnosis of dysfunctions in the economy, but cannot by themselves be regarded as a remedy.

24c Functional use

A government that wished to replace a command economy subject to physical planning and control by a market-oriented one yielding the same final physical flows or some other pre-defined set of final flows ($\grave{y}$) for which it had a preference could, in the absence of friction, rely on a centrally decreed price structure for products and factors corresponding to the desired system's eigenprices. It would need to compute these from the desired bill of final goods $\grave{y}$ by first ascertaining the gross output flows needed from the sectors, i.e. $\grave{z} = \overline{A}^{\rceil}\grave{y}$ (6.7), then computing the quota-matrix $Q = \hat{z}A\hat{z}^{-1}$ (8.3). This, in conjunction with the 'factor technology' and factor-quotas B and R, would enable it to find the cost- and norm-matrices, $C = B\overline{A}^{\rceil}$ (7.4) and $N = \hat{m}\overline{Q}^{\rceil\prime}R'$ (8.9), and hence their product, $F = CN$ (10.2). The dominant eigenvalue of the latter ϕ_*, would furnish the uniform rate of VAT ($\sigma_* = (1/\phi_*) - 1$) to be levied on each sector to generate the eigenprices of commodities ($\acute{p}$) from the eigenprices of the factors ($\acute{f}$) that emerge as the left-hand eigenvector of F corresponding to ϕ. Thus, a knowlege of the assumed technologies A, B, and $\hat{m}$ and the total factor utilization $\grave{w}$, in conjunction with the desired bill of final goods $\grave{y}$, would furnish the factor- and product-price system to be enforced in substitution for physical targets. As long as institutional arrangements could ensure the competitive character of all markets, prevent the emergence of monopoly or other 'extra-economic' friction, and maintain profit-maximizing behaviour, the price-planning could by this means achieve the result that may have eluded quantitative planners.

No doubt further analysis could reveal how price-planning of this sort could be combined with a residue of quantity-planning in certain crucial sectors, although to the extent that the latter would produce dysfunctions, the price-planners might be faced with awkward problems of the 'second-best' variety.

It should be evident from this that, short of certain coincidences between the technology and allocation scheme resulting from the final bill of goods and the consumption patterns of working households (see Chapter 22), eigenprices could have a clearer and more effective functional role than traditional 'cost-fetishist' price systems like Marxian labour-values, production prices, or the 'two-channel' prices now so much in vogue in some European people's democracies.

25
CAVEATS

Having now arrived at the end of the theoretical exposition of eigen-prices, it is essential to pass in review the qualifications, defects, and loose ends that must abound in a new concept of this kind, and have so far been mentioned only in passing, if at all. They ought to be summarized and displayed 'to better disadvantage' as a challenge to critics and improvers – without, however, claiming that anything like an exhaustive list has been achieved.

1 Eigenprices optimize nothing. They assume that the usual optimization problems have already been solved, possibly on the basis of some social welfare function that is left out of sight, with the result of yielding the technical coefficients, demand structure, and factor allocation that we observe to be at work in the economy under review. By equating product-prices to marginal costs (in terms of factor-rentals and each other) and factor-rentals to marginal revenue productivities (in terms of product-prices), they reveal a price structure that would have induced the economy to select the quantitative flows actually observed in search of an achievable optimum, and thereby give expression to the implicit view on the desirability of products and the scarcity of factors taken by the economy itself. They are thus a way of describing or explaining what *is* happening, not what *ought to* happen or what *would* happen if certain desiderata were met.

2 Eigenprices can at best measure efficiency at given levels of resource utilization. They contribute nothing to an appraisal of the economic system as a mobilizer or steward of the resources *available* to it. A system could be excellent in making the best possible use of all the resources it utilizes, but abysmal in drawing the stock of available resources into production – by keeping it idle or depleting it with reckless unconcern for the future. Indeed, the most glaring deficiencies

of present or past systems may lie precisely in their inability to secure the full or rationally full employment of resources. One may conjecture that performance in this respect will depend on the general equilibrium characteristics thrown up by various systems, their reactions to rationing situations, multiplier effects, and the propagation of disequilibria between sectors, as treated in models of 'dual-decision' hypotheses, with Drèze and Malinvaud-type equilibria. Our own model and its eigenprice structure is completely silent on all-important performance criteria of this type.

3 Eigenprices are heavily dependent on the measurement of physical flows, particularly where such flows are inferred rather than directly observable. This applies with particular force in the case of resources or factors of production whose physical flows cannot, without overstraining our conceptual apparatus, be measured independently of revenues or output values. The difficulties of measuring physical capital stock are well-known and unresolved; so are the conundrums posed by the physical measurement of 'entrepreneurship', 'skill', or 'talent'. Yet our concept of eigenprices blithely assumes that we can identify and unambiguously measure such flows as they are absorbed in various branches of production, and establish utilization coefficients and quotas on this basis. The scope that this opens up for arbitrary choice and procedures justified by mere convention may well be greater than unbiased comparisons can bear.

4 'Eigencost ratios' and 'eigenprices' depend not only on the range and nature of physical factor flows that our statistical ingenuity may have brought to light, but also on the definition of the 'rewards' (in 'factor-liras') in terms of which they are measured. Where this is only done unpurged of direct taxes, the eigencost ratios will be overestimates of the true final-use flows mortgaged to the factors, and the eigenyield correspondingly understated, possibly even to the extent of reversing its sign from positive to negative. It is doubtful, however, if any statistical basis for estimating net-of-tax factor-rewards will in practice be available for any real economy in time or space. Our comparisons will therefore inject a substantial bias against economies relying more on direct taxation for government revenue and in favour of those relying on indirect taxes. The mechanical reduction of all pre-tax factor-flows in the ratio that direct taxes bear to GNP would mitigate this, but would fail to differentiate between factor-owners, who are typically subject to widely different rates of direct taxation.

Add to this the essentially static nature of eigenprices and their inevitable vulnerability to differential errors of aggregation imported by input–output tables of different sectoral breakdown, and our elaborate edifice may well dissolve into thin air.

Should we, then, consign the concept of eigenprices without further ceremony to the dustbin of speculative theory? This must be left to the reader to judge, but we can at least claim that it is no further from operational usefulness than a host of price concepts that have profoundly influenced economic thought, and even policy, throughout historical time. It may, moreover, commend itself as a feasible attempt to overcome the limitations of a 'one-factor' world and various exclusively 'cost-based' value constructs which neglect the obvious influence of 'utility' or 'usefulness' as a cooperant element in the formation of value. It is this, in our submission, that entitles it to serious consideration and further thought.

PART III

Eigenprices: A Foray into the Real World

26
INTRODUCTION

No theoretical construct as esoteric and arcane as eigenprices must at first sight appear to be should be offered to the public without some attempt, however cursory, to test its performance as a tool of analysis for the real world, whether as a pointer to the curing of ills or merely as a diagnosis of imperfections. With this in mind, we venture to exhibit the results of two very different and qualitatively unequal experiments undertaken on the witch's brew of statistical data which the world at present has on offer.

The first of these is in the nature of a pilot survey designed to bring together a number of countries following divers policies, traditions, and ideologies, in an attempt to compare their eigenprices and surpluses at identical – or at least similar – points in time. This had to be undertaken under pressure of time and with inadequate means upon 'untreated' data, although devoted and expert help with computing facilities was generously offered and ruthlessly exploited.[1]

The dubiousness of the results will become evident as the makeshift methodology unfolds, and will be re-emphasized in fairness to the reader at as many points in the argument as concern over tedium will allow.

Substantially fewer reservations need to be entered about the second experiment, reported in the special Annex by Dr A.E. Steenge, which supplements the author's *ad hoc* 'cross-section' tests by a more intensive exploration of two particularly well-documented countries, the Netherlands and Hungary, in which a number of consecutive years could be studied, with all the additional and corrective insights that only time-series analysis can furnish. Dr Steenge's residence in the first country and extended visits to the second made it possible to penetrate further into the exact nature of the data on offer, to question their validity, and to adapt them more closely to the purpose in hand. I am therefore inclined to place greater reliance on these results than on my own, even though there is little scope for direct comparison or contradiction between the two.

However that may be, it would be misguided to regard the results of either experiment as a litmus test of the relevance or validity of eigenprices, whether in a positive or a negative sense. It would indeed be disappointing, and possibly destructive of any interest attaching to the methodology, if they did no more than confirm our preconceptions in regard to the countries under review. Some surprises and perplexities must clearly be expected, and all that can legitimately be hoped for is that the results, however much they may disturb us, should not be devoid of meaning, or so offensive to common sense as to invite instant dismissal. If that is so, we can at least claim that the first hurdle has been passed and the way is clear for the more thorough and stringent tests that must surely follow before the methodology can hope to gain acceptance.

It must be left to the critical reader to judge how this hurdle has been negotiated, but let him be fully aware that it is an exercise only to *illustrate* what could be achieved, and not to reveal where the achievement will lead us. The horse is merely showing his paces, and not completing, let alone winning, the race.

Note

1 In particular we would like to record our gratitude to Mr Colin Carpenter of the Mathematical Department of Bradford University, who fought his way through the maze of that University's uniquely rich data-base in the field of input–output statistics and put them to work in fulfilment of our intention, and to Mr Guiseppe Mazzarino of the Oxford University Institute of Economics and Statistics, who acceded to our ever-changing demands with tolerance, courtesy, and consummate skill. Particular gratitude and admiration is also due to Mr Erik Dietzenbacher of the University Groningen.

IIIa

A Pilot Survey of Eigenprices from Cross-section Data

27
THE DATA

The central statistical offices of the world have by now delivered fully articulated input–output tables (in the shape of matrices X, Y, and W) for a large range of countries, based on a bewildering variety of national accounting concepts, price systems, input definitions, etc. Their standardization and adaptation to the requirements of eigenvalue computations as proposed in this book would provide a rich vineyard in which many could fruitfully labour for years ahead. The tentative results of our pilot survey offered here are designed merely to 'test the air', to ascertain whether an off-the-cuff experiment with ill-adapted figures, taken wherever and in whatever form they happen to be conveniently available, is capable of yielding *meaningful* results, however uncertain or wrong they may later turn out to be. Our choice of countries and benchmark years was determined by nothing more than easy availability, and we have accepted the data offered in their crude form without any attempt to adjust or even interpret them where unclarity remained. When the precise meaning of data was doubtful – as in the case of 'capital services', the breakdown of imports (complementary or competitive), or the inclusiveness of exports (gross or net) – we have simply assumed that it conformed to our requirements, and set to work without further ado. Our results, displayed in the tables below, must be regarded in that light and not invested with an authoritativeness or finality to which they do not pretend.

A further jolt to the reader's confidence, if that were needed, may be administered by pointing to the fact that our present results differ substantially, and in some cases spectacularly, from those of an earlier survey on similar data undertaken some three years ago.[1] This is due partly to differences in the definitions and aggregations underlying the data-base, but partly also to erroneous interpretations by the author both of the data-base and of the procedures and subroutines used in computation.[2] Salutary though this jolt may be, readers can be assured that the particular sources of error that have come to light have now been removed, and that their doubts on this score may be laid to rest if they will be good enough to disregard the earlier results and give what credence they are willing to give to the present ones wherever discrepancies occur. Other sources of error, however, will remain and must for the time being be accepted as inevitable.

The most disturbing of these errors relates to the treatment of imports. As far as could be ascertained, few countries publish a fully articulated 'import matrix' as an integral part of their official input–output statistics. Such a matrix would show in vertical array the foreign industry of origin (producer) of each import-flow in a breakdown conformable with domestic industry, with the domestic sectors of its absorption shown laterally in the same breakdown, thus enabling imports to be classified both by 'competitive' domestic sectors (as the row-sums of the matrix) and by 'complementary' sectors into whose cost structures they enter (as the corresponding column-sums). Instead, most countries make do with a single classification, listing imports either as a single *row* in parallel with factor-inputs by domestic sector of absorption, or as a single *column* in parallel with final uses, quoted with a negative sign to reduce the row-totals of the tables from the global *availabilities* (domestic and imported supplies) of each product to the home-produced *outputs* of the relevant industries. In the latter case, of course, the remaining cells of the matrix record mixed flows of domestically produced and imported products in undisclosed proportions.

In these circumstances the statistician in search or eigenprices has two choices, both equally unpalatable:

Method I He can deal with the 'hybrid' domestic-cum-import matrix as if it were based on domestic production only, and compensate for the unknown degree of 'import inflation' affecting coefficients and quotas (A and Q) by counting only *non-imported* factor flows (in our case, wages and profits) among the primary inputs of each sector, deliberately excluding any import-row from costs in order to avoid 'double-counting'.

Method II He can delete the (competitive) import column, thereby increasing the row-sums of the table (gross outputs z) and relying on the consequent reduction in coefficients and quotas to eliminate the 'import inflation' of the X-matrix. He must then make separate allowance for import-costs by adding this column as a new (positive) row in the third quadrant of the table in parallel with domestically incurred factor-costs. In this case, of course, the breakdown of the original column by 'competitive' sector will distort the results of an exercise whose logic demands the breakdown of imports by 'complementary' (absorbing) sector.

Both of these methods will obviously vitiate the results. Unfortunately, however, there is no *a priori* criterion to determine which of them is likely to do the lesser damage. We therefore decided to use both methods in parallel, and derive some comfort from the fact that the discrepancy in the resulting eigenyields is mostly of the order of 5–10 per cent, thus only marginally affecting the pecking order of the countries under review. Nevertheless, the potentially damaging effect on measured eigenprices must be borne in mind. It can be eliminated only when a much more thorough research effort is mounted, with full support from the central statistical bureaus concerned, who will need to delve into original sources and possibly conduct supplementary surveys. In what follows we shall in the main quote the results of method I, unless a fully articulated import matrix conformable with the main input–output table is available in some form or other.

The treatment of imports is further complicated by the practice of some countries of quoting them inclusive of import duties while others record them ex-tax, thus distorting the measured eigenyield in opposite directions.

Additional pitfalls are opened up by the different pricing conventions underlying official tables, varying between 'factor-costs', 'producer-prices', 'purchasers' prices', or a mixture of the last two, with intermediate and final outputs sometimes differentially priced, thus undermining the homogeneity assumption on which all our calculations must rely.

Last, but not least, there are also variations in the size of the 'unit of observation' serving as origins and destinations of the published flows. This may disaggregate the economy into 'industries', 'commodities', or 'establishments', thus affecting intra-sector turnovers in the main diagonal of the table to an unknown and possibly arbitrary extent. Where these are diminished or eliminated altogether (e.g. by the 'industry method'), the measured output of each sector (B) is reduced, thus increasing the A-coefficients sufficiently to compensate for the omission of the main diagonal and leaving total value-added per unit output virtually unaffected. At the same time, however, the measured use of primary outputs (factors and imports) per unit output will be inflated, thus tending to squeeze the eigenyield out of existence or even reduce it to a negative ratio. It may be conjectured that it was the aggregative nature of the observation units underlying earlier data that caused negative eigenyields to appear in the case of the United Kingdom and the Federal Republic of Germany, where the present survey results in positive ratios.

Add to all this that some statistical bureaus, lacking funds or skilled manpower, substitute rules of thumbs for painstaking or costly surveys, and that these practices are often left undisclosed, and it will be clear that input–output statistics force the statistician in search of eigenprices into a minefield through which only extraordinarily fine-toothcombing or extraordinary luck can secure a passage unscathed. It must be confessed that shortage of time and resources compel us to put our trust in the second. The only alternative would have been to forgo the pilot survey altogether and present the reader with nothing but the dry bones of theory. We have chosen the more perilous, not to say 'heroic', course; but let the reader beware!

Notes

1 Francis Seton, 'A Quasi-competitive Price Basis of Intersystem Comparisons of Economic Structure and Performance', *Journal of Comparative Economics*, vol. 5, 1981, pp. 367–91.

2 For example, a sub-routine purporting to compute all the eigenvectors of a matrix was later found to yield only *right*-handed eigenvectors, where the nature of eigenprices demanded the use of *left*-handed eigenvectors for their correct computation.

28
THE PROBLEM OF AGGREGATION

It must have occurred to the reader by now that the ideal intersectoral flow table demanded by our methodology would be one in which the disaggregation of the economy went far enough to isolate production units or groupings producing no more than one homogeneous service or commodity. This might necessitate a table with anything from 250 to 1000 sectors, depending on the size and complexity of the economy. As will be seen from the first column of Table 29.1, however, the input–output tables available are consolidations of such 'basic sectors' into some 30 to 75 sector groupings whose homogeneity in the sense above it takes the eye of faith to see. A 'condensation ratio' in the region of 10:1, such as must be assumed in most of these cases, is bound to give rise to aggregation errors whose direction and size is notoriously difficult, if not impossible, to gauge. The only way in which we may hope to obtain an indication of the robustness or sensitivity of our results to such condensation would appear to be the parallel computation of our ratios and prices with data subjected to a similar degree of condensation in comparison with those presented by the original input–output tables.

We have therefore supplemented our pilot survey with a separate exercise in which all computations were preceded by 'pre-consolidating' the n 'micro-sectors' of the published tables into the 9 standard 'macro-sectors' A to I identified in the notes to Tables 29.3 and 30.1, thus applying approximately the same condensation ratio to these tables as they themselves may have been subjected to in comparison with the ideal, but unattainable, homogeneous 'base-tables'. In the tabulation below the results of this exercise are added in brackets wherever relevant immediately after the results of the 'micro-sector-based' computation derived from the original tables (or '*post*-consolidated' from these in the case of macro-sector breakdowns as presented in Tables 29.3 and 30.1). The latter are shown as unbracketed figures throughout.

As may be seen from Table 29.1, the condensation has the effect of reducing the eigencost ratio, but not by as much as would alter it out of all recognition. The most substantial aggregation error (− 18.4 per cent) occurs in the case of Italy, where the figures are in any case subject to special doubt owing to suspected imperfections in the published data. Apart from this case, the order of the economies listed remains unaffected by the condensation. We may conclude with due caution, therefore, that in this respect at least the distorting effects of aggregation, though noticeable, are unlikely to be so damaging as to make the calculation of eigenprices totally useless.

This is confirmed by the outturn of eigenprices themselves (Table 29.3), which are in general only marginally affected by pre-consolidation, although there are some notable exceptions: services (I) are overpriced ($p_0 > 1$) in Germany on micro-sector calculations, but emerge as *under*priced from the preconsolidation exercise. The same is true of agriculture (A) in the United Kingdom and household consumption in Japan, while the opposite holds for wages in relation to profits (wage–rental ratio) in Czechoslovakia. Structural eigenratios, on the other hand (Table 30.1), are totally unaffected by the condensation as far as the sectoral structure is concerned, except (marginally) in the UK and the USSR, where the condensation ratio is largest, while factor-shares show a slight shift away from wages to the surplus (eigenyield). The final use structure shows a shift towards investment in the case of Germany and towards consumption in the USSR, but is only marginally affected in other countries.

All in all, one may be tempted to conclude that the methodology is under only relatively weak threat from aggregation errors. We must however enter two caveats. Even a slight reduction in the eigencost ratio is bound to have the effect of raising the eigenyield $\sigma_* \left(= \dfrac{1}{\phi_*} - 1\right)$ very sharply, resulting, in some cases, in distortions by a factor of 2–5. It may be better therefore to give preference to ϕ over σ when quoting a characteristic parameter for various economies, even though the latter may have greater intuitive appeal.

In the second place, the disturbing effects of aggregation may not be determined by the 'condensation ratio' independently of the *level* of aggregation to which that ratio is applied. Reducing articulation in the ratio 1:9 from 80 to 9 sectors may well have different effects from reducing it in the same ratio from 700 to 80, quite apart from the fact that the effects must depend on the exact structure of the original network and the similarity or discrepancies between its several row or column structures. To that extent our supplementary exercise cannot be regarded as conclusive and the 'robustness' or eigenprice calculations under aggregation has not been firmly established. But neither has that of a large variety of input–output-based calculations which have by now gained widespread acceptance.

29
PRICE-DEVIANCE AND EIGENYIELD

Since eigenprices are defined as approximations to the perfectly competitive prices appropriate to given configurations of economic flows, one might well expect operative price systems to differ from them more radically (i.e. expect the 'price deviance' to be larger) in non-market

Table 29.1 *Ten economies in descending order of 'price-deviance' (d)**

	Articulation†	d(%)‡	Eigencost ratio ϕ_*§
Poland 1971	32	29.73	0.4652(0.4518)
USSR 1972	56	28.62	0.9545(0.8953)
Italy 1974	44	22.10	0.4143(0.3379)
Czechoslovakia 1973	40	21.47	0.6646(0.6598)
Yugoslavia 1972	29	14.52	0.9005(0.8989)
Sweden 1969	35	13.42‖	0.8646(0.7325)‖
Fed. Rep. of Germany 1970	44	12.29	0.9097(0.9026)
Japan 1970	60	12.28	0.9124(0.9061)
United Kingdom 1972	60	7.93‖	0.9627(0.8357)‖
United Kingdom 1963	73	3.78‖	0.9736(0.8622)‖

* Eigenprices computed by method I (see text) unless otherwise stated. Figures in brackets show the results of computations on pre-consolidated data (see text).
† Number of sectors distinguished in original input–output table used (n).
‡ Root-mean-square deviation of current prices from eigen prices for the n sectors of each country weighted by their GNP contributions (valued at eigenprices); i.e.,

$$d \equiv \left(\sum_1^n y_*(p_0-1)^2 \Big/ \sum_1^n y_*\right)^{1/2}$$

where p_0 is the reciprocal of the standardized eigenprice p_*, such that the coincidence of the two prices would imply $p_0 = 1$.
§ ϕ_* is the dominant eigenvalue of the 'cost-norm' matrix $F(CN)$ – see Chapter 10 and equation (10.4). Figures in brackets show the result of the same computation performed on the tables when *pre*-consolidated into the nine sectors of Table 29.3 below.
‖ Eigenprices computed by method II (see text), using 'complementary' imports as recorded in the third quadrant of the official tables.
Sources: Input–output tables supplied on tape courtesy of University of Bradford data-bank, compiled from published official sources.

than in market economies. To some extent this is borne out by the second column of Table 29.1, where the two types of economy appear in general near the top and the bottom of the table respectively. There are, however, some exceptions to this. The appearance of Italy among the East European economies may be due in part to a defective data-base, but could also reflect the presence of monopoly elements, oligopolistic practices, or non-tariff protection distorting prices away from their competitive levels as readily as total or partial abrogation of the market in favour of central planning might occasion. Similar forces may also account for the relatively large price deviance in Germany and Japan, while the highly ('competitive') pricing of the British economy emerging from the table comes as something of a surprise. Let it serve to remind us that our calculations are far too imperfect to be reliable, even though the price deviances uncovered do not fly in the face of economic intuition with sufficient force to be summarily dismissed.

Our confidence may be slightly more shaken by the behaviour of measured 'cost effectiveness' (low ϕ or high σ) as evidenced in the last column of Table 29.1 and in Table 29.2. The seemingly brilliant performance of Czechoslovakia compared with Germany and Japan is of course highly counterintuitive. It must be borne in mind, however, that

Table 29.2 *Ten economies in descending order of eigenyield* (σ)*

	Articulation†	Eigenyield σ_*(%)‡
Czechoslovakia 1973	40	50.47
Austria 1964	54	16.90‖
USA 1967§	76	16.00‖
Sweden 1969	35	15.66‖
Yugoslavia 1972	29	11.05
Fed. Rep. of Germany 1970	44	9.93
Japan 1970	60	9.60
USSR 1972	56	4.77
United Kingdom 1972	60	3.87‖
United Kingdom 1963	73	2.71‖

* Eigenprices computed by method I (see text) unless otherwise stated.
† Number of industrial sectors distinguished in published input–output table used.
‡ $\sigma_* \equiv 1/\phi_* - 1$, where ϕ_* is the dominant eigenvalue of the cost-norm matrix $F(CN)$; see text.
§ Result of earlier pilot survey; validity particularly doubtful.
‖ Computed by method II (see text), using 'complementary' imports as recorded in the third quadrant of published input–output table.
Sources: Input–output tables supplied by courtesy of University of Bradford data-bank compiled from published official sources.

Table 29.3 *Eigenprices* $(p_*)^a$ *and current pricing* $(p_0)^b$

Production sector[c]	Czechoslovakia 1973 p_*	Czechoslovakia 1973 p_0	W. Germany 1970 p_*	W. Germany 1970 p_0	Japan 1970 p_*	Japan 1970 p_0	United Kingdom 1972 p_*	United Kingdom 1972 p_0	USSR 1972 p_*	USSR 1972 p_0
A	1.116(1.098)	0.896(0.911)	1.084(1.091)	0.922(0.917)	1.090(1.077)	0.917(0.928)	0.967(1.084)	1.034(0.922)	1.110(1.097)	0.901(0.912)
B	1.170(1.164)	0.854(0.859)	0.911(0.917)	1.098(1.090)	1.016(1.032)	0.984(0.969)	1.013(1.079)	0.987(0.927)	1.041(1.056)	0.960(0.947)
C	0.859(0.842)	1.164(1.188)	0.916(0.914)	1.091(1.094)	0.961(0.934)	1.040(1.071)	0.866(0.900)	1.155(1.111)	0.992(0.967)	1.008(1.034)
D	0.937(0.878)	1.067(1.139)	0.993(1.019)	1.007(0.981)	0.933(0.908)	1.072(1.101)	0.767(0.780)	1.303(1.282)	0.910(0.906)	1.099(1.104)
E	1.044(1.056)	0.958(0.947)	1.009(1.011)	0.992(0.989)	1.013(1.003)	0.987(0.997)	0.941(0.943)	1.063(1.060)	1.034(1.030)	0.967(0.971)
F	0.912(0.856)	1.097(1.168)	0.983(1.002)	1.018(0.998)	1.013(1.014)	0.987(0.986)	0.870(0.870)	1.150(1.149)	0.770(0.803)	1.299(1.245)
G	1.019(1.002)	0.982(0.998)	0.972(0.994)	1.028(1.006)	0.994(0.989)	1.006(1.011)	0.879(0.891)	1.138(1.122)	0.953(0.959)	1.049(1.043)
H	1.071(1.068)	0.934(0.936)	0.965(0.973)	1.037(1.028)	1.001(1.007)	0.994(0.993)	1.043(1.041)	0.959(0.961)	1.084(1.073)	0.922(0.932)
I	1.071(1.073)	0.934(0.932)	0.984(1.020)	1.016(0.980)	1.007(1.011)	0.993(0.989)	1.054(1.061)	0.949(0.942)	1.085(1.097)	0.922(0.912)
Primary inputs	r_*	r_0	r_*	r_0	r_*	r_0	r_*	r_0	r_*	r_0
Wages etc.[d]	1.018(1.006)	0.982(0.994)	1.017(1.003)	0.983(0.997)	1.003(1.002)	0.997(0.998)	1.020(1.004)	0.980(0.996)	1.096(1.010)	0.912(0.990)
Profits, etc.[e]	1.016(1.015)	0.984(0.985)	0.997(0.998)	1.003(1.002)	1.011(0.999)	0.989(1.001)	1.021(1.011)	0.979(0.989)	1.045(1.002)	0.957(0.998)
Imports[f]	1.016(1.015)	0.984(0.985)	0.997(0.998)	1.003(1.002)	1.011(0.999)	0.989(1.001)	0.998(1.011)	1.002(0.989)	1.045(1.002)	0.957(0.998)
Final uses	f_*	f_0	f_*	f_0	f_*	f_0	f_*	f_0	f_*	f_0
Household cons.	0.946(0.955)	1.057(1.047)	0.963(0.997)	1.038(1.003)	1.003(0.998)	0.997(1.002)	1.008(1.003)	0.992(0.997)	0.941[l](0.962)	1.003[l](1.039)
Gvt. cons.	1.033(1.013)	0.968(0.987)	1.130(0.997)	0.885(1.003)	1.034(1.009)	0.967(0.991)	1.078(1.033)	0.920(0.968)		
Gross invest't[g]	1.070(1.060)	0.935(0.943)	0.984(0.990)	1.016(1.010)	1.005(1.057)	0.995(0.946)	1.018(1.010)	0.982(0.990)	1.097[m](1.062)	0.912[m](0.942)
Exports[h]	1.037(1.022)	0.964(0.979)	0.998(0.999)	1.002(1.001)	1.006(1.000)	0.994(1.000)	0.887(0.956)	1.127(1.046)		
Imports[i]	1.047(1.026)	0.955(0.975)	0.950(0.967)	1.053(1.013)	1.036(1.014)	0.965(0.986)	0.887(0.956)	1.127(1.046)		
Implied ratios[j]	g_*	g_0	g_*	g_0	g_*	g_0	g_*	g_0	g_*	g_0
Wage rental	1.002(0.991)	0.998(1.009)	1.020(1.005)	0.980(0.995)	0.992(1.003)	1.008(0.997)	0.999(0.993)	1.001(1.007)	0.953(1.008)	1.049(0.992)
Inv't/Household consumption	1.131(1.110)	0.884(0.901)	1.022(0.993)	0.978(1.007)	1.002(1.059)	0.998(0.944)	1.010(1.007)	0.990(0.993)	1.166[n](1.104)	0.858[n](0.906)
Gvt/Hhld cons.	1.092(1.061)	0.916(0.942)	1.173(0.993)	0.852(1.007)	1.031(1.011)	0.970(0.989)	1.078(1.030)	0.927(0.971)	1.166[n](1.104)	0.858[n](0.906)
Exp./Imp.[k]	0.990(0.996)	1.009(1.004)	1.051(1.012)	0.952(0.988)	0.971(0.986)	1.030(1.014)	0.889(1.030)	1.125(0.971)	1.166[n](1.104)	0.858[n](0.906)

Figures in brackets show the result of parallel computations on the same data in pre-consolidated form.
[a] Eigenprice per unit-worth of local currency. Computed by consolidating eigenprice-values obtained from original (disaggregated) input–output tables as left-hand eigenvector of *P* for production sectors and of *F* for factors; final-use prices obtained as ratios of total eigenvalues to current values. All prices 'scaled' to equate GNP values in the two price systems.
[b] Current price per unit-worth of eigenprice, i.e. reciprocal of p_*. [c] A = Agriculture, fishing, and forestry; B = Mining, quarrying, fuel extraction; C = Food, drink, and tobacco; D = Chemicals, plastics, rubber, etc. E = Metals and engineering; F = textiles, leather and clothing; G = Other manufacturing; H = Construction; I = Utilities, transport, trade, and services.
[d] Including wage-related compulsory insurance charges. [e] Incomes classified as 'operational surplus', assumed to be gross of depreciation charges, but excluding planned or prescribed contributions to public budgets in the nature of production taxes. [f] Imports according to the 'complementary' classification, distinguished only in countries compiling inter-industry tables based on domestic production. In countries where imports are absorbed in normal inter-industry flows, figures for imports are distinguished only in the 'competitive' classification in the form of negative final-use columns. [g] Including net increases in stocks (inventory movements). [h] Assumed to be gross of imports. [i] 'Competitive' classification. [j] Obtained by forming ratios between the relevant rows above. [k] Imports classified as 'complementary' or competitive, according to availability. [l] Total consumption. [m] Total non-consumption final uses. [n] Non-consumption/consumption.

in most centrally planned economies the division between the portion of operational surplus retained by state-owned enterprise ('profit') and the portion channelled into the state or local authority budget is determined on political or administrative grounds, such as the desired levels of bonuses to employees or the preferred degree of decentralization of investment decisions, and that the former portion is therefore far from being a true measure of entrepreneurial reward. To the extent that it is arbitrarily fixed at a low level it will of course inflate the measured 'surplus' of the economy and exaggerate σ. There is no way of correcting for this without resorting to 'price-grafting' (imposing ratios observed in other economies), which is precisely what our method is designed to avoid. It will cause less surprise to find the United Kingdom relegated to the lowest level of performance, but the position of Yugoslavia in relation to Germany and Japan is disturbing.

Most disturbing of all, however, is the zero, or even positive, correlation between price deviance and eigenyield, when it might have been expected that the more 'competitive' economies (low d) would also be the more 'cost-effective' (high σ). In large measure this may be explained by the fact, already noted in Chapter 11, that high σ is not necessarily a measure of efficiency in the technological or allocational sense, but may be achieved by depressed factor-rewards arising from political coercion, self-abnegation, or supineness on the part of factor-owners (e.g. labour unions). This need not be accompanied by the 'overpricing' of factors (wage-labour appears to be *under*priced in both Czechoslovakia and the USSR – see Table 29.3), but could be due to an imposed pattern of final demand which assigns to labour and/or other factors relatively low 'proper' rewards (eigenrentals r_0). Conversely, the low British eigenyield may be due to continued government reliance on direct rather than indirect taxation, a fact that obviously inflates current (pre-tax) factor-rewards, thereby squeezing the measured (pre-tax) surplus.

We conclude our comments on Tables 29.1 and 29.2 with the plea that, given the reservations we have repeatedly made, their findings do not invalidate the methodology by producing self-contradictory, nonsensical, or irrelevant results; and feel encouraged, with due diffidence, to advance the claim that the method seems to justify further and more detailed exploration beyond the scope of this book.

30

MEASURED EIGENPRICES AND CURRENT PRICING BEHAVIOUR

There is little internal evidence in Table 29.3 on which to test the credibility of our findings, as it gives us precisely the sort of information on which our intuition tends to be unreliable or biased. Let us therefore concentrate on the nature of these findings on the provisional assumption that they are correct reflections of reality – which we may suspect they are not.

Looking down the p_0 columns, we find that agriculture (A) is consistently underpriced by a small margin, with the exception of UK agriculture, where pre- and post-consolidation procedures give opposing verdicts. Food processing (C), on the other hand, is consistently overpriced by a larger margin, though less so in the USSR. The chemical industry (D) is overpriced by as much as 28 per cent in the UK, much less so everywhere else, and more or less 'correctly' priced in Germany. Engineering (E), on the other hand, is underpriced everywhere except in the UK, while textiles and clothing are underpriced in the market economies and overpriced in Eastern Europe, presumably because of their orientation towards household consumption. Construction (H) is underpriced everywhere except in Germany, while utilities and services (I), somewhat surprisingly, are consistently underpriced.

Among the primary inputs, labour is generally given its 'correct' price, except for Czechoslovakia and the USSR, where there is a slight degree of underpricing.

Household consumption goods are generally slightly overpriced (except in the UK), goods and services entering government consumption appear to be underpriced, while investment goods are generally underpriced by an even larger margin. Not surprisingly, export goods are assigned prices within 1 per cent of the 'correct' level, except for Czechoslovakia, which underpriced them by some 3–4 per cent, and the UK, which overpriced them by nearly 5 per cent.

The wage–rental ratio is very slightly inflated compared with the 'correct' level in the UK and Czechoslovakia, and slightly depressed everywhere else. The widely quoted underpricing of investment goods relatively to consumer goods is slight but noticeable (about 10 per cent) in both the USSR and Czechoslovakia, while the opposite bias is evident in the market economies other than Japan.

In all cases, the deviation of current prices from eigenprices is so small as to be almost insignificant, and doubts have been expressed whether, in these circumstances, the whole elaborate exercise is worth undertaking at all.[1] While we have considerable sympathy with readers who resent being taken through so many hoops only to find themselves where they started, we would like to plead the following in our defence.

Even if eigenprices turned out to be identical with current prices in every respect ($p_* = 1$ in every case), the resulting legitimization of current prices would not be an idle undertaking; for their 'correctness' could not have been known and proved without this exercise. The disenchantment with such an outcome could be likened with the annoyance of a book keeper who checks a long addition of figures and regrets having done so because the addition turns out to have been correct in the first place.

It should also be noted that the observed closeness between current prices and eigenprices emerging from this survey is evident only when eigenprices are 'post-consolidated' into the 9 macro-sectors we have distinguished – a process in which major discrepancies are 'averaged out'. When the comparison is between the original *micro*-price structures, even the average discrepancy varies from 4 to nearly 30 per cent (see *d*-column in Table 29.1), while the eigenprices of individual microsectors may deviate from the current price level by as much as a factor of 4 or 5.

Indeed, a few micro-sectors show a pronounced tendency to overpricing in more than one country, and some of the practical usefulness of our method may lie precisely in pinpointing these (see Table 30.1) in order to provide restrictive practices courts in market economies or price reform commissions in centrally planned economies with prima facie evidence on the direction that further investigation could fruitfully take.

Table 30.1 *Cases of substantial 'overpricing'* ($p_0 > 1.5$)*

	Czs.† 1967	Czs.† 1973	FRG‡ 1970	Ity§ 1974	Jpn 1970	Pol. 1971	Swd. 1969	UK 1963	UK 1972	USSR 1972
Agr., forestry, fisheries				3.447						
Iron and Mg ore	1.904									
Crude oil and gas			2.280	3.752						
Petrol refining		1.806					2.695	3.282	3.280	
Meat and preserves				4.535						
Milk and dairy prods				2.870						
Grain milling								1.658		
Sugar								2.380		
Veg. and animal fats	1.538								1.901	1.871
Other foods										1.871
Bevs & alcohol. drinks					1.594					
Tobacco		5.173	2.716	4.785	2.582					
Non-ferrous metals	1.526						1.556			
Metal prods, machinery and equip't						1.700				
Air and sea transport									1.694	
Construction						1.926				
Recreational and cultural market services				2.141						
Lodging and catering				1.949						

* Current price over 50 per cent above eigenprice.
† Czechoslovakia.
‡ Federal Republic of Germany.
§ Italy.

Note

1 G. Szakolczai, in the Discussants' Comments on the author's paper presented at the IEA conference in Athens, October 1981, shortly to appear in the Conference Proceedings, edited by D. Hague. See also Szakolczai's comments on the translated paper (in Hungarian) in Csikós-Nagy Béla and Szakolczai György (eds), *Alkalmazkodás az új árviszonyokhoz,* Budapest, 1983.

31
STRUCTURAL EIGENRATIOS

Owing to the closeness of macro-eigenprices to current price structures already noted in the last chapter, the structural ratios of various economies in the breakdown shown in Table 31.1 are only marginally affected by the consolidation and are entirely unaffected by further consolidation in the first three countries quoted.

More radical discrepancies would of course be pointed up if we disaggregated economies down to the original micro-sectors, but their number is in most cases too large to be conveniently accommodated in the format of this book. Suffice it to say that the range of discrepancies between current and eigenprices (p_0) reaches from 0.9 to 3.3 in the British economy of 1972, and from 0.8 to 2.7 in the case of the Federal Republic of Germany. This must imply a very radical revision of structural ratios in the wake of condensation for at least some micro-sectors.

Table 31.1 *Structural eigenratios in various economies (%)* (The structure of GNP)†*

	Czechoslovakia 1973	W. Germany 1970	Japan 1970	UK 1972	USSR 1972
Sectoral share‡					
A	12.5 (12.5)	3.9 (3.9)	6.7 (6.7)	2.5 (2.9)	23.8 (23.6)
B	6.7 (6.7)	6.5 (6.5)	2.3 (2.3)	2.5 (2.7)	8.6 (8.7)
C	3.6 (3.6)	3.3 (3.2)	2.5 (2.5)	3.7 (3.6)	5.3 (5.3)
D	5.4 (5.4)	5.2 (5.2)	3.5 (3.5)	3.8 (3.7)	4.0 (4.0)
E	27.8 (27.8)	17.7 (17.7)	17.6 (17.6)	15.3 (15.0)	20.3 (20.3)
F	5.7 (5.7)	3.0 (3.0)	2.8 (2.8)	2.9 (2.9)	4.2 (4.3)
G	4.6 (4.6)	4.8 (4.8)	1.0 (1.0)	4.1 (4.1)	5.9 (5.9)
H	14.8 (14.8)	10.4 (10.4)	8.1 (8.1)	7.2 (7.1)	12.8 (12.8)
I	19.9 (18.9)	45.1 (45.1)	55.5 (55.5)	58.0 (58.1)	15.1 (15.2)
Primary input shares					
Wages, etc.§	39.1 (38.6)	53.7 (53.0)	41.8 (41.8)	58.1 (57.2)	53.2 (49.8)
Profits, etc.‖	27.4 (27.4)	37.3 (37.3)	49.4 (48.8)	26.7 (26.4)	42.2 (40.5)
Imports¶				3.8 } (16.4)	} (10.5)
Eigenyield**	33.5 (34.0)	9.0 (9.7)	8.8 (9.4)	11.4 }	4.6 }
Final-use structure					
H'hold consumption	46.8 (47.3)	55.6 (57.5)	53.6 (53.7)	46.5 (46.2) }	58.7‡‡ (60.1)
Govt consumption	12.7 (12.4)	14.2 (57.5)	8.4 (8.2)	19.6 (18.6) }	
Gross investment	37.6 (37.2)	29.9 (30.1)	37.9 (45.1)	16.4 (16.3) }	41.3§§ (39.9)
Exports (net of imports)	33.5 (33.2)	20.5 (20.5)	11.3 (11.2)	17.5 (18.9) }	
Other††	− 30.6 (− 30.1)	− 20.2 (20.5)	− 11.2 (− 18.2)	−	

* Figures in brackets show the result of parallel computations on the same data in pre-consolidated form.

† In Czechoslovakia and the USSR the gross national product (GNP) is replaced by the 'Net Material Product' (NMP) in all calculations, thereby excluding from GNP the value of all final services insofar as not contributed by materials 'embodied' in them.

‡ A = Agriculture, fishing, and forestry; B = Mining, quarrying, fuel extraction; C = Food, drink, and tobacco; D = Chemicals, plastics, rubber, etc.; E = Metals and engineering; F = Textiles, leather, and clothing; G = Other manufacturing; H = Construction; I = Utilities, transport, trade and services.

§ Including wage-related compulsory insurance charges.

‖ See footnote e to Table 29.3.

¶ See footnote f to Table 29.3.

** Share of eigenyield in GNP/NMP, i.e. $\sigma_*/(1 + \sigma_*)$.

†† Losses, items of defence expenditure, and other final uses NEM.

‡‡ Total 'consumption'.

§§ Total 'non-consumption'.

32
FURTHER EXPERIMENTS WITH EIGENPRICES

It is interesting to note that the dispersion of eigenprices and their reciprocals (d on average) varies less between the countries under review than the skewness of their distribution among the micro-sectors in each economy. The skewness of p_0 is indeed most pronounced in many economies, implying the existence of three or four micro-sectors 'exploiting' a much larger number of downstream sectors and final users through the 'overpricing' of their products by a factor of 3 or more. As an example, Table 32.1 shows the relevant distribution for the British economy in 1972.

Table 32.1

Current pricing p_0	Number of micro-sectors	Proportion of GNP
0.8 –	2*	0.3040
0.9 –	17	0.3480
1.0 –	20	0.1855
1.1 –	9	0.0991
1.2 –	6	0.0306
1.3 –	2†	0.0075
1.4 –	1‡	0.0017
1.5 –	–	–
1.6 –	1§	0.0210
1.7 –	–	–
1.8 –	–	–
1.9 –	1‖	0.0004
2.0 –	–	–
3.0 –	1¶	0.0020

*Retailing, Public admin./Dom. service/Ownership of buildings.
†Sugar, paper and board.
‡Non-ferrous metals other than aluminium.
§Transport other than road and rail.
‖Oils and fats.
¶Petrol refining.

Similar distributions apply to what might be called the 'sectoral trade-terms' (t_0), defined as the ratio between output-pricing (p_0) and the analogous pricing of inputs (say, q_0) which measure the 'net' or 'total' exploitation by a sector of the rest of the economy (downstream and upstream) by overpricing its sales and, possibly, gaining 'unfairly' from the (average) underpricing of its purchases. This variable, which is the analogue of 'effective protection rates' in international trade, might well repay further study, but will not be investigated here as it is outside the scope of this book.

A good deal of interest also attaches to the precise sectoral pattern of 'overpricing' in various economies and on the characteristic of sectors that tend towards under- or over-pricing. Cursory forays in this direction have led me along several false trails, of which only one will be mentioned here for purposes of illustration. It was found, for instance, that overpricing was positively correlated with labour intensity in all market economies except the UK, but negatively correlated in all the East European economies under review, although none of these correlations (except those of Poland and the UK) were significant even at the 10 per cent level. There was, in addition, some positive correlation between overpricing and 'consumer orientation' (as measured by the proportion of sectoral output going to household consumptions) in all the countries investigated, but only the correlation coefficient for Italy and Czechoslovakia turned out to be significant (at the 5 per cent level). Again, the correlation between sectoral trade terms (t_0) and consumer orientation turned out to be (insignificantly) positive in all countries except Italy, where it was negative, but a positive correlation between overpricing and 'material intensity' (proportion of non-factor to total input costs) can be reported for all economies except Sweden, with significant results at the 10 per cent level in Czechoslovakia, Italy, Japan, and the USSR, and at the 5 per cent level in Poland. The results are too weak, of course, to allow firm conclusions of any kind; they do, however, indicate the direction in which further research might go.

Enough has now been said in our submission to justify the hope that in the concept of eigenprices we have hit upon a tool of analysis that bids fair to yield interesting, relevant, and, dare one hope, significant results if used with due caution for the diagnostics of economic systems or countries and the comparative study of their structures and performance.

IIIb

Time-series Analysis for the Netherlands and Hungary

(*Special Annex contributed by Dr A.E. Steenge,*
University of Groningen)

33

INTRODUCTION

It is well-known that prices in centrally planned or socialist economies have different functions to fulfil than in market economies. Here the debate on 'functional' (policy-geared) prices versus 'diagnostic' prices (aiming to reflect social relations, whether actual or idealized) is of great relevance.[1] It might be considered, for instance, that prices should stimulate the production of qualitatively superior goods and discourage that of outdated products, or that they should stimulate the introduction and use of new technologies. Thus, on the one hand, they must be high enough to cover production costs and secure appropriate profit rates, but not so high as to discourage the use of alternative technologies which might become available shortly thereafter.[2]

To highlight price differences in planned and market economies a number of economic models have come into use, of which linear models are probably the most popular, because of their rich history in inter-system comparisons. One of the most serious defects of existing models, however, is their total neglect of demand factors, which deprives them of the capacity to reflect real-world scarcities. Moreover, these models fail to provide suitable criteria for the efficiency with which inputs are used. If, for example, the factor capital is used inefficiently in a particular sector, the model being used may simply adjust prices in order to enable that sector to obtain the same rate of profit on capital as others without signalling the defect. Further difficulties arise from the lack of comparability of basic statistics, e.g. the conformity of Western input–output tables with the System of National Accounts (SNA), in contrast to East European tables, which mostly follow the MPS (Material Product System).[3]

The system presented here is designed to fill an important gap in synthesizing 'cost-fetishism', which imputes total value to one or more primary factors, with 'use-fetishism', which derives factor-rentals from the value of final products. The synthesis is achieved by the use of left-hand eigenvectors corresponding to the dominant eigenvalues of certain matrices appearing in linear transformations (see Part I above). If the relevant matrices have no eigenvalue equal to unity, this signalizes the existence of an 'eigenyield' or 'eigensurplus', positive or negative, extracted from the factors by (or acquired by them from) an – as yet – unspecified agency (foreign countries, monopolists, future generations, the state, or simply 'others').

Seton proposed his system primarily as a tool for international comparison of structural characteristics and performance criteria and took the first tentative steps towards empirical testing, which are supplemented in greater detail in the following chapters. Some of the results are easy enough to interpret, while others need further attention. The general picture, however, promises well for the potential interest of the method.

The relevance of eigenprices for international comparison would no doubt be documented most clearly if it could be shown that different economic systems tended to exhibit different eigenprice structures, so that the revealed structure could be used as a basis for systemic classification at any point in time. A necessary condition for this would be that the annual fluctuations in the eigenprice profile of a particular country should not be so large as to obscure systemic differences from other countries. To test for this condition, we must of course trace the development of eigenprices in a number of different years in contrasting economies, in order to highlight how different economies coped with emerging disequilibria, thereby revealing systemic peculiarities which might remain hidden in a simple cross-section analysis at a given point in time.

In what follows we present two empirical studies, one for a Western-type country, the Netherlands, and one for a socialist centrally planned economy, Hungary. We calculated eigenprices and eigensurpluses for the Dutch postwar economy 1948–78, using data compiled by the Central Bureau of Statistics (Centraal Bureau voor de Statistiek) (CBS). During this period the organizational framework of the economy remained substantially unchanged, although the share of government increased from roughly one-third to about two-thirds of the national income without, however, resulting in a substantial increase in government intervention in the private sector. The importance of the foreign sector also remained roughly constant. We may expect, therefore, that a study of eigenprices implying the over- and underpricing of specific flows in terms of current prices will provide information on the time-profile typical of a medium-sized open economy based on free enterprise with some elements of state control.

In the case of Hungary, we analysed the period 1970–9, using tables prepared by the Central Statistical Office of that country (Központi Statisztikai Hivatal). This period is of considerable interest, as it is the period of the 'second wave of reforms'.[4] The New Economic Mechanism (NEM) of 1968 resulted in systemic changes of considerable scope by East European standards. After the 1968 reform, the system of planning directives was abolished altogether and enterprises were given a relatively free hand in determining their output and cost structure. The planning agencies still drew up the national plan as usual, but this plan was no longer broken down to enterprise level. Central policy was imposed on lower échelons through economic regulators instead of administrative command. The NEM did not quite fulfil the aspirations of 1968. After a temporary recourse to centralization during the years 1973–7, the period 1979–80 again saw considerable changes, particularly the adoption of 'competitive market prices'.[5] At the same time, the Hungarian system had to cope with the world price shocks in the field of energy and other resources, and to grapple with worsening balance of payments problems.

A comparison of the two systems is therefore of special interest. Both countries are medium-sized; both experienced an agricultural phase followed by a period of rapid industrialization. Holland is a member of the EEC and OECD, while Hungary is a member of the CMEA, and since 1982 also of the IMF. We start with a brief discussion of the economic background of both countries, followed by the presentation of the data, and conclude with a number of observations on the method in the light of this.

The author of this annex is particularly indebted to Francis Seton for discussions and comments on an earlier draft. Special thanks are also due to Andrew Bródy of the Institute of Economics of the Hungarian Academy of Sciences for providing the opportunity for a stay of several months at the Institute. He also wishes to thank Ferenc Bánhidi of the Hungarian Central Planning office, György Szakolczai of the Econometric Laboratory of the Institute of Economics, and György Molnar, also of the Institute of Economics of the Hungarian Academy of Sciences, for providing additional information on the Hungarian economy. For the processing of the Dutch data, thanks are due to Erik Dietzenbacher of the Econometric Institute of the University of Groningen, and to Jaap Stellingwerff for help at an earlier stage. Financial support from the Netherlands Organization for the Advancement of Pure Research (ZWO) is gratefully acknowledged.

Notes

1 F. Seton, 'The Question of Ideological Obstacles to Rational Price Setting in Communist Countries', in Alan Abouchar (ed.), *The Socialist Price Mechanism*, Duke University Press, Durham, NC, 1977.

2 For such and other observations see e.g. G. Fink, 'Price Distortions in the Austrian and in the Hungarian Economy', *Zeitschrift für Nationalökonomie*, vol. 41, 1981, and *Preisverzerrungen und Unterschiede in der Produktionsstruktur zwischen Östtereich und Ungarn*, Studien über Wirtschaft-und Systemvergleiche, Springer-Verlag, Vienna and New York, 1981.

3 After 1968, national income accounting in Hungary was extended to include the value of services as well. However, minor discrepancies between the Hungarian system of national accounts and the United Nations system remain. See *Hungary: An Economic Survey*, Occasional Paper 15, International Monetary Fund, Washington DC, 1982.

4 The terminology is borrowed from W. Brus, 'The Eastern European Economic Reforms: What Happened to Them?' *Soviet Studies*, vol. 31, 1979.

5 J. Kornai, 'Comments on the Present State and Prospects of the Hungarian Economic Reform', *Journal of Comparative Economics*, vol. 7, 1983.

34
BRIEF CHARACTERIZATION OF THE POSTWAR DUTCH ECONOMY

As in most other West European countries, several stages can be quite easily distinguished in the postwar economic development of the Netherlands. A fairly common division is the following one into four periods.[1]

34.1 Reconstruction and recovery, 1945–50

Economic damage, both national and personal, wrought by the war was enormous. Material damage alone was estimated at 25 billion guilders at current prices.[2] However, recovery was fast owing to a number of favourable circumstances. In the earliest postwar years, employers and employees were prepared to accept strong government intervention in the form of strict wage, credit, and foreign currency controls; social harmony was a decisive factor here. Another factor was the substantial American support given in the form of Marshall aid in 1948. Each year large portions of the growth in national income could be invested in industry. This guaranteed rapid industrialization, which could absorb the growing working population and help to compensate for the loss of the colonial empire in South-East Asia. The policy of strict wage controls ensured the country's favourable position in foreign markets. Commodity exports almost doubled in the period 1948–50 (from 2.8 to 5.5 billion guilders), while national income increased by 28 per cent (from 13.4 to17.1 billion guilders in 1950). The balance of payments still remained weak, however, owing to the persistence of grave shortages of all kinds. The whole period was characterized by a rapid transformation from a traditional type of society based on agriculture, trade, and services to a modern industrial economy. Particularly fast expansion was registered in the production of metals, chemicals, and food, while trade and services remained important.

34.2 Recovery and expansion, 1950–63

This rapid industrialization policy continued throughout the period. In the early 1950s, most economic controls were lifted. According to the Dutch Central Bank, the recovery period was completed by about 1953 in the monetary sphere. However, a strict wages policy remained a cornerstone of national policy and was a major factor in keeping inflation down to 2–3 per cent per annum. Equally important was the fact that Dutch firms had become highly competitive in foreign markets. Exports were concentrated on Western Europe, with the German Federal Republic emerging as the largest trading partner. The balance of payments showed surpluses year after year, a process mitigated only by the appreciation of the guilder by 5 per cent in 1961. But two consequences of the national policy orientation became obvious only gradually. In the first place, because of the relatively low level of wages, industrialization was extensive rather than intensive in comparison with neighbouring countries. Textiles become less competitive than before, followed somewhat later by metals. In the second place, owing to the strong concentration on exports, domestic consumption was squeezed, creating a large overhang of postponed demand. This, combined with general excess demand for labour, gave rise to various 'grey' and 'black' markets to overcome disequilibria, and to an influx of foreign workers from southern Europe. However, overall growth continued and national income almost trebled. Social security legislation greatly expanded, leading among other things to a significant raising of old-age pensions in 1957 (the 'AOW' law).

34.3 Growth and reorganization, 1963–74

In 1963 tensions in the labour market became so serious that the policy of wage controls had to be abandoned. The breakdown of the system resulted in explosive wage increases. Nominal wages rose by 17 per cent in 1964, increasing real wages by 10 per cent. Profits then rapidly fell in a number of already weakened sectors such as textiles, metals, and other labour-intensive branches. A period of reorganization and restructuring ensued, characterized by shutdowns, takeovers, and mergers, which changed Dutch industry fundamentally. For a time, newer developments in expanding sectors such as electronics, information-processing, transport, trade, and government services were able to take over the role of traditional industries in providing employment for the still growing population. Towards the 1970s, however, it became clear that the newer branches would not be able to absorb all those seeking employment, and 'industrial innovation' became the keynote of the current debate. Growth in industrial investment came to a stop fairly abruptly in 1971, and in the following year trade unions called attention to the necessity of maintaining employment for the first time.

During the period 1963–74 as a whole, the rate of inflation doubled from 4 to 8 per cent per annum, showing an average rate of 5.6 per cent, while national income, investment, and labour productivity still continued on their fast upward trend. The balance of payments, however, became weak, mainly because of overconsumption. Thus unemployment became an issue only at the beginning of the 1970s. Government expenditure rose faster than national income, with its share rising from 40.8 per cent in 1964 to 53.7 per cent in 1974.

34.4 Reorganization and stagnation, 1974

The first oil crisis was a turning point for the Netherlands, as it was everywhere else. The government reacted with restrictions on expenditure on fuels of every kind combined with wage and price controls. In 1974 and 1975 the growth in national income slowed down, while unemployment rose apace. (The number of unemployed, already 100,000 in 1972, passed the 200,000 mark in 1975.) Anti-cyclical measures failed to bring unemployment down, but the rate of inflation remained high and reached 10.2 per cent in 1975, while budget deficits increased. After 1975, the Keynesian approach gave way to policies of a more monetary kind, and public expenditure was cut significantly in the hope of reducing the still rising deficit. This brought about a slowdown in inflation but increased the number of unemployed, thus increasing the pressure on the social security system. In the wake of the second oil crisis and other causes, the economy stagnated in the late 1970s, and growth rates turned negative in the 1980s: by the end of 1981, about 400,000 people were unemployed. Public expenditure had to be cut once again, causing further changes in wages policy (with specially severe effects in the public services) and in the social security system. Thanks to the export of large quantities of natural gas, however, the balance of payments went into persistent surplus. This, of course, had the effect of strengthening the guilder and adversely affecting the less competitive sectors of the economy.

Notes

1 Here we follow broadly the classification of W. S. P. Fortuyn, *Kerncijfers 1945–1983 van de sociaal-economische ontwikkeling in Nederland*, Kluwer, Deventer, 1983. Another source is J. P. Windmuller and C. de Galan, *Arbeidsverhoudingen in Nederland*, 3rd edn, part 2, Het Spectrum, Utrecht/Antwerpen, 1979.

2 This compares with a national income (net, market prices) of 13.4 billion guilders in 1948, the first year for which detailed national accounts are available, when the government budget was 4.0 billion guilders (in 1975 prices). See Fortuyn, op cit., pp. 14–15, and *Tachtig jaren statistiek in tijdreeksen 1899–1979*, Centraal Bureau voor de Statistiek, 's Gravenhage, Staatsuitgeverij, 1979, p. 144.

35

EIGENPRICES FOR THE NETHERLANDS, 1948–78

Our calculations are based on yearly input–output tables published by the Dutch Central Bureau of Statistics (CBS).[1] The original tables were based on a breakdown into 30 odd sectors following standard international classification. Substantial changes in the CBS classification occurred in 1969 in regard to the oil and gas sector; until 1969 oil and gas exploration and exploitation activities were recorded under 'Chemicals', while in subsequent years these activities were recorded under a separate heading. At about the same time, because of the shutdown of the Dutch mines in the province of Limburg, coal-mining virtually disappeared as an economic activity. The CBS sought to overcome a discontinuity in the time series of input–output tables by publishing two figures for the year 1969, labelled 1969^1 and 1969^2 in Tables 35.1–35.4, where the latter stands for the new classification.

A further break in the series occurred in 1969, when the tables were adapted to the introduction of the value-added tax (BTW), which replaced earlier turnover taxes. The main difference with previous usage was that indirect taxes paid on final deliveries were now recorded in the corresponding columns of the fourth quadrant. (This was the case for both the series 1969^1 and 1969^2 mentioned above.) No set of figures was published for 1971.

To facilitate comparison with the pilot survey in this book and to avoid the excessive detail of the CBS classification, we have aggregated the tables into nine 'macro-sectors' (henceforth to be called 'sectors' *tout court*):

A Agriculture, forestry, and fishing
B Mining, oil, and gas
C Food, drink, and tobacco

D Chemicals
E Metals and engineering
F Textiles, leather, and clothing
G Other manufacturing
H Construction
I Utilities, transport, and services.

Primary input categories were aggregated into three:

1 Wages and salaries (including employers' contributions to social security)
2 Other incomes (profits, dividends, etc.)
3 Imports of commodities and services (c.i.f.)

This classification leaves the 'τ-row' to record the sum of all indirect taxes and price-decreasing subsidies. The above-mentioned CBS shift in the classification of the oil and gas activities corresponds to a shift from sector D to B in the aggregation. Above we also mentioned the break in the CBS publications regarding the taxes on final purchases, starting from 1969. We have adhered to this in the aggregation scheme, because of the impracticality of recalculating figures according to the pre-1969 schedule. For the numerical consequences of this, refer to the tables and the next chapter.

Note

1 Central Bureau voor de Statistiek, *De produktie-struktuur van de Nederlandse volkshuishouding*, various years, 's Gravenhage, Staatsuitgeverij, and *Nationale rekeningen*, various years, 's Gravenhage, Staatsuitgeverij.

Table 35.1 *Sectoral eigenprices for the Netherlands, 1948–78.*

	Sector*								
Year†	A	B	C	D	E	F	G	H	I
1948	1.145	0.953	1.029	0.974	1.019	1.011	1.010	1.003	0.953
1949	1.138	0.983	0.966	0.990	1.034	1.029	1.022	1.019	0.970
1950	1.051	0.980	1.002	0.987	1.038	1.036	1.021	1.020	0.964
1951	1.048	1.009	1.000	0.980	1.039	1.027	1.019	1.017	0.969
1952	1.047	1.041	0.962	0.981	1.041	1.022	1.024	1.023	0.990
1953	1.040	1.032	0.968	0.996	1.039	1.023	1.021	1.027	0.984
1954	1.045	1.035	0.979	1.005	1.037	1.025	1.019	1.023	0.976
1955	1.050	1.019	0.976	0.996	1.024	1.025	1.013	1.016	0.985
1956	1.052	1.019	0.978	0.997	1.017	1.046	1.007	1.012	0.984
1957	1.083	1.006	0.986	0.983	1.017	1.050	1.009	1.010	0.980
1958	1.119	1.007	0.979	0.972	1.016	1.047	1.007	1.008	0.984
1959	1.077	1.009	0.970	0.972	1.022	1.047	1.015	1.013	0.989
1960	1.085	1.007	0.971	0.976	1.025	1.048	1.015	1.013	0.983
1961	1.096	1.012	0.968	0.979	1.029	1.053	1.019	1.018	0.978
1962	1.078	1.018	0.961	0.975	1.033	1.053	1.021	1.019	0.982
1963	1.077	1.016	0.965	0.973	1.035	1.056	1.022	1.020	0.981
1964	1.080	1.012	0.972	0.958	1.036	1.056	1.023	1.022	0.978
1965	1.065	1.015	0.961	0.975	1.038	1.061	1.025	1.027	0.978
1966	1.045	1.020	0.964	0.961	1.041	1.062	1.028	1.031	0.979
1967	1.046	1.028	0.976	0.984	1.041	1.049	1.027	1.029	0.974
1968	1.038	1.053	0.981	0.966	1.041	1.051	1.026	1.030	0.976
1969^1	1.003	1.022	0.979	0.948	1.042	1.030	1.027	1.025	0.989
1969^2	1.002	0.835	0.978	1.036	1.042	1.032	1.024	1.024	0.987
1970	1.004	0.857	0.993	1.029	1.034	1.028	1.020	1.023	0.986
1971	n.a.	n.a.	n.a.	n.a.	n.a.	n.a.	n.a.	n.a.	n.a.
1972	1.003	0.853	0.987	1.022	1.031	1.028	1.020	1.024	0.993
1973	1.006	0.874	1.009	1.014	1.026	1.023	1.015	1.019	0.991
1974	1.010	0.928	1.003	1.010	1.023	1.020	1.013	1.016	0.994
1975	1.000	0.939	0.992	1.010	1.024	1.025	1.015	1.018	0.996
1976	1.004	0.957	1.001	1.007	1.021	1.021	1.012	1.015	0.993
1977	1.007	0.947	1.014	1.010	1.025	1.026	1.017	1.020	0.989
1978	1.006	0.937	1.018	1.010	1.026	1.025	1.017	1.021	0.989

*A = Agriculture, forestry and fishing; B = Mining and oil; C = Food, drink and tobacco; D = Chemicals; E = Metals and engineering; F = Textiles, leather and clothing; G = Other manufacturing; H = Construction; I = Utilities, transport, and services.

†1969^1 = old classification, 1969^2 = new classification (see text); data for 1971 are not available.

Table 35.2 *Eigenprices (primary factors) and eigenyield for the Netherlands, 1948–78.*

Year	Factors* 1	2	3	Eigenyield† (σ in %)
1948	0.996	1.007	1.005	8.03
1949	1.001	1.004	1.001	9.71
1950	1.000	0.997	1.007	9.77
1951	1.000	0.997	1.006	9.87
1952	1.004	0.998	1.001	9.90
1953	1.003	0.997	1.003	9.72
1954	1.002	0.997	1.004	9.52
1955	1.001	0.999	1.002	8.68
1956	1.001	0.999	1.002	8.06
1957	1.000	1.000	1.002	7.08
1958	1.001	1.003	0.999	6.79
1959	1.002	1.001	0.999	7.41
1960	1.001	1.001	1.001	7.37
1961	1.002	0.999	1.003	7.78
1962	1.003	0.998	1.003	7.94
1963	1.002	0.997	1.004	8.03
1964	1.002	0.998	1.004	8.05
1965	1.003	0.996	1.005	8.42
1966	1.003	0.995	1.005	8.81
1967	1.002	0.995	1.006	9.18
1968	1.002	0.996	1.006	9.71
1969[1]	1.004	0.996	1.002	3.55
1969[2]	1.006	0.997	1.001	3.40
1970	1.005	0.997	1.001	3.34
1971	n.a.	n.a.	n.a.	n.a.
1972	1.006	0.997	0.999	3.70
1973	1.004	0.996	1.001	3.11
1974	1.004	0.998	0.998	2.67
1975	1.005	0.995	0.999	2.73
1976	1.003	0.996	1.000	2.31
1977	1.003	0.995	1.003	2.79
1978	1.003	0.995	1.003	2.81

*1 = Wage factors; 2 = Other factors; 3 = Imports.
† $\sigma = 100(1/\phi - 1)$, where ϕ = eigencost ratio.

Table 35.3 *The GNP by origin in eigenprices, the Netherlands 1948–78**

	Sector†								
Year	A	B	C	D	E	F	G	H	I
1948	8.52	0.15	17.59	3.85	10.45	9.79	3.23	9.77	36.66
1949	7.44	0.12	18.93	4.15	10.90	10.55	2.85	9.41	35.65
1950	5.84	0.12	20.18	5.54	11.27	11.22	2.96	8.39	34.48
1951	5.40	0.14	20.02	6.49	12.93	10.04	3.47	8.35	33.17
1952	5.90	0.14	19.61	6.69	13.62	8.08	2.84	8.77	34.37
1953	5.03	0.10	19.42	6.72	13.72	8.44	2.68	10.20	33.70
1954	5.40	0.12	19.12	6.86	14.35	8.11	2.84	9.19	34.02
1955	5.09	0.12	17.85	7.00	15.12	7.91	2.91	9.40	34.61
1956	4.94	0.14	16.98	7.40	15.00	7.78	2.72	9.95	35.09
1957	4.94	0.12	16.69	8.31	14.71	7.49	2.66	10.35	34.73
1958	5.24	0.12	17.42	8.29	14.09	6.72	2.67	10.13	35.34
1959	4.76	0.12	17.00	8.21	14.95	6.74	2.83	10.28	35.12
1960	5.16	0.11	16.19	8.68	16.05	6.74	3.04	9.86	34.19
1961	4.86	0.11	15.63	8.52	16.18	6.90	3.05	10.41	34.35
1962	4.76	0.11	15.07	8.41	16.47	6.57	2.98	10.32	35.33
1963	4.23	0.11	15.46	8.05	16.19	6.89	3.08	10.32	35.68
1964	4.36	0.11	15.12	7.66	16.31	6.62	3.08	11.75	35.00
1965	4.39	0.10	14.56	8.08	16.21	6.16	3.14	11.94	35.43
1966	3.89	0.13	14.53	7.98	15.82	6.17	3.16	12.68	35.66
1967	3.76	0.17	14.84	8.12	15.14	5.23	3.10	13.46	36.18
1968	3.50	0.32	14.42	8.46	15.16	5.17	3.12	13.72	36.13
1969[1]	3.63	0.40	13.74	9.02	16.48	4.99	3.30	11.97	36.47
1969[2]	3.17	2.91	14.42	6.50	15.58	5.29	3.36	12.21	36.56
1970	2.94	3.47	13.99	6.26	16.36	4.50	3.32	12.10	37.07
1971	n.a.	n.a.	n.a.	n.a.	n.a.	n.a.	n.a.	n.a.	n.a.
1972	2.99	3.63	13.58	6.19	15.57	4.07	3.29	12.38	38.30
1973	3.21	4.23	13.60	6.54	15.66	3.72	3.38	11.54	38.13
1974	2.59	6.87	12.61	8.20	16.07	3.32	3.42	9.98	36.95
1975	2.56	6.85	13.01	6.34	15.05	2.89	3.06	10.28	36.97
1976	2.91	7.72	12.44	6.74	14.84	2.70	3.11	9.94	39.60
1977	2.75	7.13	11.65	5.66	13.91	2.45	3.06	10.30	43.09
1978	2.65	6.35	11.50	5.49	13.47	2.33	3.06	10.77	44.38

*Sectoral shares in value-added, neglecting factor services rendered directly to final users (fourth quadrant of input–output table).
†For the definition of the sectors, see Table 35.1.

Table 35.4 *The GNP in eigenprices by factor share and final use, the Netherlands, 1948–78**

	Factor†			Final use‡				
Year	1	2	3	*Pc*	*Gc*	*Gi*	*Ex*	*Oth.*
1948	32.31	35.29	24.96	56.01	2.45	13.92	23.72	3.89
1949	30.78	36.39	23.99	54.66	2.08	13.89	27.74	1.63
1950	28.76	34.34	28.00	49.86	2.04	12.80	32.13	3.17
1951	27.23	33.21	30.58	45.68	2.69	11.99	36.12	3.52
1952	27.94	34.52	28.54	45.61	3.30	12.05	39.01	0.04
1953	28.19	34.95	28.00	44.83	3.56	13.78	37.64	0.19
1954	28.51	34.46	28.33	44.08	3.42	13.45	36.73	2.32
1955	28.78	35.37	27.86	43.36	3.51	14.40	37.23	1.51
1956	29.12	34.29	29.13	43.13	3.77	15.32	36.59	1.20
1957	30.06	33.99	29.35	41.90	3.42	15.76	37.30	1.62
1958	31.61	34.21	27.82	43.81	3.02	14.60	38.13	0.45
1959	30.88	34.38	27.84	42.97	2.49	15.44	38.91	0.20
1960	30.87	34.57	27.71	41.21	2.55	15.13	39.50	1.61
1961	32.46	33.13	27.19	42.13	2.53	15.45	38.08	1.81
1962	33.22	32.55	26.87	42.65	2.75	15.53	38.02	1.06
1963	34.20	31.35	27.01	43.30	2.96	12.42	38.07	0.25
1964	34.57	31.05	26.93	41.54	2.79	16.77	37.20	1.70
1965	35.64	30.94	25.65	42.30	2.46	16.95	37.30	1.00
1966	36.94	29.46	25.50	42.47	2.57	17.84	36.44	0.68
1967	37.12	30.04	24.43	42.89	2.70	18.45	35.92	0.05
1968	37.06	29.73	24.37	42.12	2.50	18.93	36.16	0.28
1969[1]	39.54	30.76	26.27	41.06	2.46	15.90	38.89	1.68
1969[2]	40.17	30.11	26.43	40.52	2.42	16.19	39.24	1.64
1970	40.78	28.56	27.43	39.49	2.48	16.38	40.43	1.22
1971	n.a.	n.a.	n.a.	n.a.	n.a.	n.a.	n.a.	n.a.
1972	41.98	28.96	25.49	39.45	2.60	16.10	41.77	0.08
1973	42.15	28.71	26.12	38.57	2.46	15.34	43.09	0.54
1974	40.53	26.35	30.52	36.17	2.47	13.47	46.69	1.20
1975	43.23	26.02	28.09	39.31	2.89	13.35	44.83	−0.37
1976	41.52	27.76	28.46	38.65	2.80	12.32	45.83	0.39
1977	41.62	29.03	26.64	41.30	2.59	14.31	41.51	0.30
1978	42.50	29.30	25.47	42.29	2.67	14.82	39.99	0.23

*As in Table 35.3 the GNP neglects factor services rendered directly to final users (the fourth quadrant of the input–output table).

†1 = Wage factors; 2 = Other factors; 3 = Imports; $1 + 2 + 3 + 100(1 - \phi) = 100$, where $\phi = 100/(100 + \sigma)$. (For σ see Table 35.2).

‡*Pc* = Personal consumption; *Gc* = Government consumption; *Gi* = Gross investment; *Ex* = Exports; *Oth.* = Other. *Pc* + *Gc* + *Gi* + *Ex* + *Oth.* = 100.

36

DISCUSSION OF THE RESULTS FOR THE NETHERLANDS

Tables 35.1–35.4 summarize the results for the Netherlands for 1948–78. Recalling that an eigenprice below unity implies overpricing of the commodity or factor in terms of current prices, and an eigenprice above unity a corresponding underpricing, we may call attention to a few especially interesting features.

Tables 35.1 suggests that agricultural production was underpriced throughout the postwar period, although the degree of underpricing appears to have diminished steadily, possibly reflecting the improved organization of agricultural interests in the late 1960s and 1970s. The relatively large underpricing in 1948 and 1949 may reflect the government's efforts to keep down the prices of primary products in the immediate postwar years. The jump in eigenprices in 1969 can be attributed to the aforementioned shift in the recording of the value-added tax on final deliveries. The economy's eigenyield having fallen under the post-1969 tax registration schedule to somewhat more than 3 per cent, agriculture has approximately the 'right' proportion of indirect taxes under the new scheme. (The same is valid, *mutatis mutandis*, for other sectoral eigenprices for 1969 and following years.) The data of the table also suggest an inverse correlation between the eigenprices of sector A and the food-handling and processing activities represented largely in sector C. For the latter sector, the picture is complicated by the qualitative differences between its constituent commodities. A more detailed breakdown may easily give substantially different results.

Sectors B and D could also be viewed in conjunction, as they might be even more complementary than A and C. It appears that up to 1969 the basic primary products of sector B were underpriced, while the processing activities of sector D were overpriced. The substantial change evident in 1969 may be traced to the shift in classication affecting the oil and gas industry which is known to favour monopolistic elements; from then on we note that the over- and underpricing of the two sectors is reversed. The effects of re-classifying the oil and gas sector are also interesting from a purely statistical point of view. Sector B's eigenprice falls from 1.022 to 0.835, while that of sector D rises from 0.948 to 1.036, a considerably smaller change. This is due largely to the fact that the total output of sector B in 1969 was 1.4 billion guilders under the old classification while that of sector D was 15.9 billion. Under the new classification, however, the same figures were 7.0 and 10.0 billion guilders respectively. Thus, 'overvalued' oil and gas account for some four-fifths of sector B's output under the new classification. In the year designated 1969[1], the effect of these over-valued commodities on the eigenprice of sector D was exerted by only about one-third of its output-mix.

Another interesting feature is the behaviour of these eigenprices for 1974 and the years immediately following. Contrary to what one might expect, we observe a *rise* in the eigenprice for sector B, from 0.874 to 0.928 in 1974. That is, there is *less* measured overvaluation in the period of the severe oil price shocks. The reason for this may be found in the fact that sector B's imports (mainly oil) more than doubled (from 5.9 billion guilders in 1973 to 14.4 billions in 1974), while indirect taxes increased only moderately (from 2.1 to 2.2 billion). The other relevant entries in the third quadrant also increase, but much less than (the value of) imports. Thus, the entry in the τ-row decreased in proportion to the totality of the primary factors, which entails an increase in eigenprice.

As for the typical manufacturing sectors E–H, the table suggests a tendency to underpricing, which may be the result of greater competitiveness in these sectors and a lack of concerted action by the interests concerned. The systematic overpricing of sector I (eigenprices below unity), on the other hand, may be indicative of a substantial degree of government participation in the revenues of this sector through taxation; it is also in line with the lack of competitiveness of public utilities in the Netherlands.

Table 35.2 appears to indicate fewer and less radical changes through the years, but nevertheless presents interesting features. There is a slight, but systematic, underpricing of the wage-factor; but it is interesting to note that the wage restraint shown by labour in the recovery period (late 1940s and early 1950s) is not reflected in the data. This may reflect the fact that consumption goods were broadly 'correctly' priced in relation to the amount of labour 'embodied' in them. We also note that the wage increases of 1963 and subsequent years do not entail any significant fall in the eigenprice for labour. Perhaps the tentative conclusions drawn for the earlier period of wage restraint may apply here also, *mutatis mutandis*.

The eigenyield concept seems to provide a good indicator for cyclical phenomena. For example, the recession of 1957–8 is reflected in a fall in eigenyield, signalling a decline in indirect tax revenues. The same is possibly true for 1974 and following years, although here the situation is complicated by the changed treatment of final purchases. Furthermore, we may observe that, during the recession of 1958–9, both labour and 'other incomes' become underpriced when compared with 1957. This is consistent with a degree of oversupply of production factors, such as is typical of a recession. Imports, on the other hand, became overpriced in 1958, reflecting a stable and relatively high level of demand for foreign goods and services. However, this switch from over- to underpricing in the non-labour factor of production is not in evidence in the recession following the oil-price increase of 1973. This may be due to the considerable change in general conditions that had taken place. While the recession triggered off by the cost-push of 1973 brought immediately increased revenues to the oil-processing companies, no such phenomenon had occurred in 1958–9. This is documented by the overpricing during the years following 1973. Later years, however, again saw a gradual erosion here.

Tables 35.3 and 35.4 were included to show the effects of eigenprice calculations on the structure of the gross national product, in line with the results of the pilot survey presented in Chapters 27–32. Table 35.3 shows the structural shifts in the Dutch economy during the period under review. The fact that the eigenprices of the traditional sectors (textiles, metals, etc.) stabilized from the late 1960s onward may point to the disappearance of the less efficient enterprises in these sectors, while the surviving firms were operating under 'normal' competitive conditions. Table 35.4 shows the breakdown of GNP according to factor-shares and final use structure.

The pronounced discontinuity in the time-series for sectors B and D points up the sensitivity of the results to sectoral aggregation of the crude data. The same is valid for changes in tax schedules, as is illustrated by the contrast in eigenyields for the pre-1969 years and the later years. It should be noted in conclusion that eigenrentals of factors of production are in general very close to unity – a finding that evidently needs to be put on the agenda for future research.

37

A BRIEF CHARACTERIZATION OF POSTWAR HUNGARY

The Hungarian People's Republic, when launched in 1949, introduced a centrally planned economic system. This meant that five-year plans spelled out interim targets for important economic aggregates in the necessary breakdown, while annual and quarterly plans provided a detailed disaggregation down to enterprise level. Firms were given specific directives on output, investment, wages, prices, and employment, and all inputs were centrally allocated. In this system, prices had in the main no more than an accounting function, and generally did nothing to reflect demand or supply conditions in the markets for goods or factors. Producer and consumer prices were fixed at a level determined by a large variety of turnover taxes and subsidies. International price movements had little influence on domestic price developments, as the discrepancy between foreign and domestic prices was covered largely by financing out of special funds.[1]

From the very beginning, major efforts were made to establish a firm industrial base for the country's development. The centrally planned system met with a measure of success, particularly in the 1950s when resources were being extensively reallocated. Very high rates of investment were realized, and as a consequence output, employment, and industrial capacity grew rapidly, signalling the onset of a period of extensive growth in these early years. With the exhaustion of labour supplies, however, further economic growth became dependent on the increasing productivity of an almost static labour force.[2] Economic pressures arising from this dictated a change from extensive to more intensive growth policies. However, the formulation of plans that were both flexible and sufficiently detailed became an increasingly complex task, largely dependent on up-to-the-minute statistical reporting of high quality; and their implementation was hampered by the general lack of incentives for workers and management alike.

To alleviate the administrative burden of central agencies, a full-scale consolidation of enterprises into larger units was initiated in the early 1960s. In a series of mergers, the number of state industrial enterprises was reduced from over 1300 in 1961 to some 850 in the mid-1960s. But this heavy concentration of industry had adverse effects on the production of consumer goods, semi-finished products, and spare parts, which was dependent mainly on small- and medium-size enterprises.[3] Moreover, Hungary's limited domestic market and its relative lack of natural resources encouraged an increasing orientation towards Western markets. With some 50 per cent of the national product going to exports and one-third of this dependent on hard-currency areas, industry had to be organized so as to be geared to the demands of foreign trade and export promotion. The flexibility that this required was difficult to achieve within a tightly organized central planning system. It was generally accepted by the mid-1960s, therefore, that only a fairly thorough reform of the system would guarantee the country's future economic performance.

The second wave of reforms that followed took about two years to prepare; the 'New Economic Mechanism' (NEM) came into force on 1 January 1968, with an overall package of measures. The scope of centralized price determination was reduced, domestic prices of exports and import-substitutes were linked to world market prices, and a major part of investment decisions was decentralized. Annual plans ceased to be enforced by direct instructions to enterprises, and were implemented indirectly by means of 'regulators'. To facilitate this, producer prices were recalculated to reflect domestic and foreign costs more accurately than before. The degree of plan-fulfilment became less decisive as a factor in determining workers' premia, yielding place to the profits of the firms that employed them. Moreover, the division of enterprise profits remaining after tax into a 'sharing' fund and a 'development' fund brought about a certain degree of decentralization in wage determination and investment decisions.

When the NEM was introduced, a number of 'brakes' were built in to mitigate the shock of the transition from the previous system. In essence, there were three price categories operative in the system: a fixed-price category (prices set directly by the government); a flexible-price category (prices fluctuating between officially set upper and lower limits); and a free-price category (prices determined largely by market forces). Controls were removed mainly on producer prices, although consumer prices were affected as well. However, even the 'free' prices were subject to a certain amount of control through general rules linking them to costing and profit margins, through the continued regulation of wages and raw material prices, and through limitations deriving from the government's wish to avoid excessive price adjustments.[4] Operative prices were regularly examined by the price control authorities.

The main form of government intervention in producer prices was the wide range of taxes and subsidies that continued to be negotiated between the government and individual enterprises. After the reform of 1968, consumer prices overtook producer prices in the case of industrial goods, but remained below them in the case of foodstuffs, transport, communication, and a number of services which continued to be subsidized via the state budget.

The intention was gradually to eliminate restrictions. But during the early 1970s the system was partially modified in the reverse direction, i.e. away from the market. The main reason for this was the intention to prevent large income inequalities, excessive labour turnover, and over-investment at enterprise level. Initially, these changes were introduced in response to a number of shortcomings that had emerged during the implementation of the new system. However, the policy responses to the external shocks were frustrated by the inflationary boom of 1972–3 and the world recession of the mid-1970s. The deterioration of the Hungarian terms of trade after 1973 led to reduced reliance on the market mechanism, and to a certain return of central direction and government intervention. By 1974, for instance, over two-thirds of the increase in world market prices was compensated for by subsidies on imports. The price disparity was particularly large for crude oil, whose domestic price remained well below the world market price for several years. However, since intra-CMEA trade prices are normally fixed annually at the level of a five-year moving average of world market prices, the price of oil imports from the USSR – Hungary's main supplier of oil – rose steadily towards the international level.

Notes

1 For an extended discussion of the institutional characteristics, we refer to J. Kornai, *Economics of Shortage*, vols A and B,

North-Holland, Amsterdam, 1980. For a recent economic survey see the earlier mentioned International Monetary Fund study, *Hungary: An Economic Survey*, Occasional Paper 15, IMF, Washington, DC, 1982. Other references include P. Hare, H. Radice and N. Swain (eds), *Hungary: A Decade of Economic Reform*, George Allen & Unwin, London, 1981; E. A. Hewett (ed.), 'Hungary: The Third Wave of Reforms', *Journal of Comparative Economics*, vol. 7, 1983; and P. Mihályi, 'Das Ungarische Modell', *Osteuropa Wirtschaft*, Volume 28, 1983.

2 Hare *et al.*, *Hungary: A Decade of Economic Reform*, p. 5.

3 Here it may be interesting to quote W. Brus, 'The Eastern European Economic Reforms: What Happened to Them?', *Soviet Studies*, vol. 31, 1979, p. 259: 'One of the elements which should secure the required degree of control under conditions of various degrees of devolution of economic authority was thought to be a higher level of organizational concentration. It we take the schematic three-tier organization of industry (ministry; intermediate – most frequently branch – organization; enterprise), it was the status of the intermediate organization which, sooner or later, was enhanced. In the course of this development the intermediate organizations underwent in some cases substantial transformation: in Hungary, where amalgamation of existing enterprises preceded the reform, the amalgamated units took over the name of enterprises, underlining the fact that the function of enterprises, with all their enhanced autonomy, became vested in these units.'

4 *Hungary: An Economic Survey*, p. 9.

38

EMPIRICAL RESULTS FOR HUNGARY, 1970–9

Our eigenprice calculations for Hungary are based on 26 sector input–output tables published by the Central Statistical Office (Központi Statisztikai Hivatal).[1] It is evident that these tables were compiled with an eye to the interests of the immediate users operating within the Hungarian economic system. Ideally, we should have processed tables conforming to the definitions of economic activities current in international practice, where the various subdivisions of light industry are aggregated into a single sector and building activities are similarly condensed. While this is the proper breakdown for most decentralized production systems, it does not correspond to the needs of the Hungarian set-up. Hungarian enterprises operate under the jurisdiction of larger economic organizations which play a dominant role in preparing production plans, dealing with parallel échelons in other industries, 'bargaining' with central authorities, etc. Many of these organizations comprise both horizontally and vertically related production stages. Accordingly, Hungarian input–output tables embody a compromise between the 'branch-type' and the 'administration-type' systems of classifying enterprises, designed to facilitate subsequent aggregations into either of these two classification schemes, as the need may dictate. In the case of building, for example, the table specifies not only 'building proper', but contains separate entries for building in agriculture, railway construction, water works, and construction activities carried out in various organizations directly financed by the state. Thus, to obtain an overview of the entire building industry, these entries can be summed up to give a reasonably accurate picture, while alternative aggregations will allow the activities of administrative divisions to be supervised. The latter subdivision can focus on the centres of integrated supply-planning, smoothing out seasonal fluctuations in revenue, centred on self-supporting entities arising from cross-subsidization, etc.

For our purpose aggregation according to the administrative principle is to be preferred. In the first place, many of the data are available exclusively in this breakdown. (This refers particularly to primary inputs, for which the 'branch-type' breakdown is usually missing.) In the second place, the computations for planning purposes usually follow the organizational classification, with the Ministry of Finance and the Planning Office distributing available funds in conformity with it. Given the dominant role of the administrative principle, it seems appropriate to analyse price patterns in accordance with the classification that flows from it.[2]

In our classification scheme, we distinguish the following administrative sectors:[3]

1 Mining
2 Electricity
3 Metals
4 Machinery
5 Building materials
6 Chemicals
7 Light industry
8 Food
9 Construction
10 Agriculture
11 Forestry
12 Transport and telecommunications
13 Domestic trade
14 Foreign trade
15 Water supplies
16 Personal and economic services
17 Health, social, and cultural services
18 Communal and administrative services

The input–output tables are in current producer prices; i.e., the entries record the receipts of producers rather than the (usually different) payments made by the purchasers, while final demand is also recorded in producer prices.

The quantitative estimate of eigenprices and eigenyield is critically dependent on the availability and quality of the data supposedly representing the current remuneration of each primary factor. Given that Hungary followed a strict wages policy, the identification of the rewards of the factor 'labour' causes no special difficulty, and the same should apply to the primary factor 'imports', *mutatis mutandis*. When it comes to the factor 'capital', however, a strict application of the rules of Part I is a delicate matter, mainly because of the important role played by 'bargaining' in determining the financial position of the enterprise, when 'bailing out' in the face of adverse results is an ever-present possibility.

In trying to overcome the problems involved, we resorted to alternative aggregation schemes. In the first instance, we identified the variable w_1 with the remuneration of labour including social security payments paid by employers, the variable w_2 with the totals of pretax profits and amortization, and the variable w_3 with the sum of ruble and non-ruble imports. This relegates to the residual τ-row a number of headings, such as price discounts or price premia on the use of home-produced goods and various subsidies and taxes on imports and exports, as well as additional corrections connected with the difference between producer and consumer prices (Table 38.1).

The great flexibility of the theoretical framework of Part I enables us also to incorporate certain degrees of 'hardness' into our calculations. In the second exercise, therefore, we dispensed with the pre-tax profits in row w_2 except for amortization, thereby relegating the flow of 'net profits' to the τ-row. This must result in the Frobenius eigenvalue of the ensuing system measuring not the eigenyield as strictly defined in Part I, but the surplus yielded to the reduced factor-complement 'labour, imports, and amortization'. We have thereby eliminated a source of error arising from the 'bargaining skill' of enterprise management in dealing with the central authorities rather than from truly economic effort or performance, even though this has been achieved by narrowing the scope of true primary factor-inputs to a subset of those that the economy may be presumed to require. The results of this exercise are recorded in Table 38.2, which follows the same sector classification as the previous table.

As a further step, we aggregated the 18 sectors of the first tables into 9 macro-sectors, following, as far as possible, the sector classification used for the Netherlands in Chapters 34–6 and the analysis of the pilot survey. Table 38.3, which shows the results, defines these sectors by letter in a footnote to the table. Finally, to test the effects of further aggregations, we added yet one more exercise in which the system is condensed into five major sectors (see Table 38.4).

Table 38.1 *Hungarian eigenprices for 18 macro-sectors (on standard factor-base)*

Sectors*	1970	1971	1972	1973	1974	1975	1976	1977	1978	1979
1	0.917	1.095	1.113	1.135	1.169	1.009	0.865	0.855	0.883	0.899
2	0.901	0.950	0.955	0.946	0.915	0.936	0.871	0.885	0.839	0.872
3	0.858	0.866	0.878	0.894	0.864	0.925	0.909	0.898	0.861	0.854
4	0.900	0.909	0.925	0.929	0.903	0.924	0.897	0.889	0.888	0.889
5	0.887	0.941	0.909	0.897	0.892	0.940	0.918	0.899	0.925	0.938
6	0.870	0.880	0.884	0.898	0.985	0.894	0.811	0.820	0.837	0.846
7	0.941	0.949	0.967	0.958	0.984	0.939	0.940	0.931	0.932	0.944
8	1.080	1.026	1.015	0.971	1.035	1.039	1.060	1.113	1.081	1.086
9	0.940	0.948	0.946	0.953	0.938	0.955	0.944	0.930	0.952	0.960
10	1.131	1.132	1.106	1.117	1.134	1.110	1.103	1.113	1.121	1.120
11	1.004	1.012	1.005	0.987	0.965	0.988	1.031	1.018	1.044	1.034
12	0.926	0.925	0.927	0.931	0.929	0.919	0.954	0.950	0.958	0.977
13	0.877	0.852	0.852	0.864	0.844	0.925	0.906	0.904	0.939	0.938
14	1.187	0.951	0.900	0.956	0.837	0.778	0.799	0.741	0.725	0.781
15	0.986	1.014	1.017	1.022	0.994	1.013	1.044	1.018	1.038	1.039
16	1.327	1.385	1.430	1.501	1.411	1.494	1.598	1.564	1.479	1.436
17	1.058	1.074	1.078	1.097	1.092	1.081	1.127	1.120	1.137	1.117
18	1.012	1.011	1.012	1.012	0.982	0.982	1.030	1.005	1.011	1.006
Primary factors†										
1	1.020	1.020	1.017	1.018	1.018	1.019	1.024	1.024	1.026	1.025
2	1.015	1.018	1.022	1.026	1.019	1.023	1.043	1.041	1.029	1.028
3	0.700	0.680	0.706	0.715	0.722	0.721	0.704	0.692	0.671	0.723
Eigenyield (σ in %)	11.53	14.38	14.24	12.65	10.29	10.53	16.33	12.58	15.23	13.56
Price deviance (%)	10.88	10.83	10.69	11.03	11.32	10.72	13.28	13.90	12.85	12.20

*1 = Mining; 2 = Electricity; 3 = Metals; 4 = Machinery; 5 = Building materials; 6 = Chemicals; 7 = Light industry and other; 8 = Food; 9 = Constructions; 10 = Agriculture; 11 = Forestry; 12 = Transport and telecommunication; 13 = Domestic trade; 14 = Foreign trade; 15 = Water supplies; 16 = Personal and economic services; 17 = Health, social and cultural services; 18 = Communal and administrative services.

†1 = Wage factors; 2 = Other factors; 3 = Imports.

Table 38.2 *Hungarian eigenprices for 18 macro-sectors (on reduced factor-base)**

Sectors†	1970	1971	1972	1973	1974	1975	1976	1977	1978	1979
1	1.017	1.105	1.154	1.198	1.215	0.984	0.930	0.897	0.914	0.931
2	0.827	0.860	0.858	0.881	0.876	0.932	0.901	0.914	0.851	0.896
3	0.854	0.883	0.904	0.896	0.830	0.924	0.941	0.958	0.896	0.894
4	0.806	0.810	0.815	0.821	0.783	0.799	0.804	0.780	0.787	0.800
5	0.865	0.890	0.852	0.871	0.865	0.888	0.876	0.881	0.891	0.908
6	0.826	0.845	0.844	0.875	0.986	0.882	0.816	0.836	0.850	0.867
7	0.913	0.912	0.921	0.943	0.976	0.907	0.911	0.925	0.920	0.926
8	1.118	1.067	1.062	1.009	1.102	1.121	1.119	1.170	1.151	1.154
9	0.901	0.899	0.890	0.898	0.871	0.889	0.900	0.884	0.888	0.893
10	1.251	1.244	1.247	1.224	1.257	1.248	1.238	1.230	1.238	1.241
11	0.992	1.024	1.041	1.020	0.962	1.001	0.999	1.007	1.018	1.004
12	0.950	0.965	0.989	0.986	0.980	0.986	0.979	0.981	0.979	0.992
13	0.657	0.674	0.669	0.687	0.663	0.714	0.730	0.735	0.737	0.739
14	0.638	0.664	0.603	0.616	0.543	0.504	0.623	0.546	0.545	0.654
15	1.012	1.046	1.068	1.075	1.085	1.113	1.139	1.113	1.108	1.119
16	1.114	1.098	1.092	1.113	1.053	1.112	1.102	1.066	1.077	1.063
17	1.231	1.257	1.270	1.308	1.293	1.281	1.319	1.326	1.340	1.307
18	1.209	1.237	1.271	1.301	1.264	1.280	1.299	1.298	1.269	1.262
Primary factors										
1	1.052	1.051	1.052	1.050	1.054	1.054	1.060	1.060	1.060	1.057
2	1.028	1.028	1.030	1.031	1.037	1.040	1.041	1.041	1.041	1.039
3	0.700	0.683	0.711	0.722	0.735	0.733	0.713	0.702	0.681	0.732
Eigenyield (σ in %)	57.54	61.06	62.12	64.35	58.47	58.69	65.16	63.79	64.91	59.63
Price deviance (%)	19.31	18.69	19.11	18.61	20.95	19.91	19.03	20.24	20.05	18.83

* Net profits being imputed to the τ-row (see the text). Primary factors now are: 1 = Wage factors; 2 = Amortization; 3 = Imports.
† We have followed the sectoral classification of Table 38.1.

Table 38.3 *Hungarian eigenprices for nine macro-sectors*

Sectors*	1970	1971	1972	1973	1974	1975	1976	1977	1978	1979
A	1.134	1.136	1.114	1.122	1.140	1.114	1.111	1.120	1.129	1.126
B	0.918	1.040	1.033	1.037	1.046	0.988	0.900	0.885	0.915	0.928
C	1.088	1.036	1.027	0.980	1.045	1.049	1.074	1.127	1.096	1.098
D	0.873	0.882	0.888	0.900	0.990	0.903	0.828	0.837	0.856	0.862
E	0.896	0.908	0.925	0.928	0.902	0.932	0.912	0.903	0.897	0.894
F	0.909	0.925	0.951	0.943	0.977	0.937	0.944	0.940	0.943	0.956
G	1.014	1.019	1.031	1.011	1.031	0.977	0.979	0.967	0.962	0.966
H	0.956	0.968	0.970	0.977	0.960	0.970	0.959	0.945	0.965	0.973
I	1.008	1.002	1.007	1.020	0.989	1.012	1.043	1.029	1.031	1.036
Primary factors										
1	1.017	1.016	1.013	1.013	1.012	1.013	1.016	1.017	1.017	1.018
2	1.000	1.000	1.000	1.001	0.998	0.999	1.004	1.006	1.004	1.005
3	0.701	0.682	0.710	0.717	0.725	0.725	0.709	0.696	0.676	0.728
Eigenyield (σ in %)	12.17	15.25	15.34	13.87	11.32	11.65	18.12	14.20	16.54	14.63
Price deviance (%)	8.27	7.29	6.02	6.18	6.96	6.09	8.06	9.09	8.46	8.45

* A = Agriculture, fishing and forestry; B = Mining and oil; C = Food, drink, and tobacco; D = Chemicals; E = Metals and engineering; F = Textiles, leather and clothing; G = Other manufacturing; H = Construction; I = Utilities, transport, and services. Primary factors are as in Table 38.1.

Table 38.4 *Hungarian eigenprices for five macro-sectors*

Sectors*	1970	1971	1972	1973	1974	1975	1976	1977	1978	1979
A	0.943	0.946	0.954	0.941	0.963	0.952	0.931	0.941	0.932	0.935
B	0.955	0.954	0.953	0.955	0.945	0.957	0.948	0.937	0.956	0.963
C	1.123	1.125	1.105	1.114	1.123	1.105	1.105	1.116	1.118	1.113
D	0.933	0.897	0.896	0.902	0.878	0.904	0.919	0.908	0.928	0.943
E	1.121	1.138	1.157	1.182	1.145	1.166	1.237	1.222	1.197	1.175
Primary factors										
1	1.019	1.020	1.019	1.022	1.018	1.020	1.025	1.023	1.024	1.021
2	1.000	1.000	1.001	1.004	1.001	1.001	1.012	1.011	1.008	1.006
3	0.699	0.685	0.713	0.720	0.724	0.726	0.709	0.694	0.675	0.728
Eigenyield (σ in %)	12.17	14.92	14.83	13.21	10.98	11.18	17.31	13.77	16.10	14.40
Price deviance (%)	8.09	8.88	8.75	9.59	8.84	8.67	10.85	10.41	9.97	9.15

* A = Industrial sectors; B = Construction; C = Agriculture; D = Productive services; E = Other services. Primary factors are as in Table 38.1.

Notes

1 Központi Statisztikai Hivatal, *Ágazati kapcsolatok mérlege 1970–1979*, Budapest, 1981. Another source of information was the *Statisztikai Évkönyv 1980* (Statistical Yearbook 1980) from the same publisher.

2 For example, sector 10 (Agriculture) is the result of merging the following headings in the original tables: 'Agriculture', 'Food processing activities in agriculture', 'Other industrial activities in agriculture', 'Building activities in agriculture', and 'Commercial activities in agriculture'. Sectoral nomenclature will mostly speak for itself; however, a few remarks seem in order. 'Mining' includes the exploitation and processing of Hungarian oil and gas, bauxite, etc.; refining of domestic and imported oil is registered under 'Chemicals'. The construction of highways and railways is entered under 'Transport and telecommunication'. 'Domestic trade' includes hotels and restaurants, catering services, travel agencies and the like. By 'Foreign trade' is meant the organization of import–export-related activities. 'Personal and economic services' include housing facilities, insurances, banks, repairs, etc.

3 The sectoral numbering follows established Hungarian practice. We have followed this practice to avoid confusion with the nine-sector classification we used for the Netherlands, and to facilitate the exposition of the various aggregation schemes we have employed.

4 In terms of the classification of Table 38.1, we have: A = sectors 10 and 11; B = sectors 1 and 5; C = sector 8; D = sector 6; E = sectors 3 and 4; F = part of sector 7; G = remaining part of sector 7; H = sector 9; I = sectors 2 and 12–18.

5 In terms of the classification of Table 38.1, we have: A = sectors 1–8; B = sector 9; C = sectors 10 and 11; D = sectors 12–15; E = sectors 16–18.

39

DISCUSSION OF THE RESULTS FOR HUNGARY

Although in the Hungarian case aggregation took place along administrative and organizational lines, conclusions regarding the associated products or product groups emerge quite naturally. A first impression is that our results reveal substantial differences between the eigenprices calculated for the Netherlands and for Hungary. In contrast to Holland, the Hungarian eigenprices appear to show greater variations between commodities and commodity groups, generally with fairly revealing time-profiles.

This is certainly the case for the first sector quoted in Tables 38.1 and 38.2. In the first half of the 1970s energy became increasingly underpriced in relation to the pricing of other activities within the economy. This may be traced to the fact that more than two-thirds of the increase in world market prices was neutralized through subsidies on imported goods, where the price divergence was particularly large for crude oil. Keeping the domestic price of oil low was helped, naturally, by the slow adaptation of official CMEA prices for energy to developments in other markets (more than 80 per cent of Hungarian oil is imported, mostly from the USSR). This is possibly also a factor in explaining the declining trend in eigenprices for electrical energy (sector 2) until 1975. The sudden impact of the increase in world market prices is probably reflected by the relatively high eigenprice for Chemicals (sector 6) in 1974, about half of its imports stemming from Western countries; though still indicative of overpricing, it is markedly higher than in previous – and later – years. (The same is true, though to a lesser extent, for sector 7, Light industry.)

A number of price adjustments occurred in the years 1975–6, following general world trends. Producer prices were raised by about 10 per cent in 1975 and by another 4 per cent in 1976, the largest revisions affecting the prices for energy and raw materials. To a certain extent this is reflected in the data for these years. In Table 38.1 we observe a *fall* in eigenprices for basic sectors such as Mining and Chemicals, and a *rise* for their users such as Metals, Machinery, and Building materials. In the subsequent years the pattern that developed was more or less maintained. The shift in energy prices in 1975 and 1976 is also reflected in the eigenprice of the second sector quoted, reflecting as it does the significant increase in electricity prices in a fall from 0.936 in 1975, to 0.871 in 1976 and 0.839 in 1978. (Producer prices for electricity were substantially increased both in 1976 and 1978.)

Eigenprices for Food and Agriculture reflect underpricing throughout the period, which is consistent with observations from many other sources. Moreover, a number of services still financed from the state budget are typically underpriced. The exception here is Foreign trade, which is grossly overpriced. However, this need not surprise us, since the eigenprices of these services reflect substantial margins in the import–export trade. The outcome for sector 12 (Transport and telecommunications) is something of a surprise, showing an eigenprice that seems too low in view of the fact that this sector (like Communal and administrative services) is supposed to operate on a non-profit basis.

Overall consumer prices rose by 5 per cent in 1976, almost double the average increase per annum during the previous five years. Given that wages were lagging behind prices, the rise in the eigenrental for the wage factor need not surprise us. The calculated values of 'Other factors' (in essence, the factor capital) are comparable with those of labour; with wages linked to enterprise profits through various devices, the simultaneous increase in the eigenprice for 'Other factors' in 1976 is not surprising either. The fact that our tables reflect pre-tax situations need not detract from their interest, as a supplementary 'post-tax' exercise with tax rates assumed to vary between 40 and 60 per cent, revealed no significant changes in either commodity or factor-eigenprices. Accordingly, its results are not quoted here.

Imports are largely overpriced in comparison with the other primary factors, a result that may reflect the various devices used in import–export trade. (Because of the presence of multiple price arrangements between the CMEA countries, an analysis in terms of ruble and non-ruble imports might have been interesting. This, however, would have required more extensive material.) The relatively high eigenyield figure for 1976 seems consistent with the picture drawn above. We would also point out that the observed eigenyields are of the same order of magnitude as those emerging from the pilot survey in the case of Austria, Sweden, and Yugoslavia. The two aggregation exercises distinguishing nine and five macro-sectors respectively, confirm our results in broad outline, again *mutatis mutandis*.

Price-deviances (for definition see Table 29.1) are seen to be quite sensitive to aggregation or to the changing factors (inclusion or exclusion of net profits from the factor base). The fact that in our tables aggregation decreases deviances is not surprising, as the sectoral differences will have a tendency to average out. The exclusion of profits will affect especially the sectors that use some of the primary factors in relatively small amounts, such as certain services where amortization and imports are of relatively minor importance. Here a shift of profits to the τ-row will decrease the proportion of the remaining primary factors in the value-added components to a greater than average extent. The consequences for the eigenprice of those sectors may be expected to be larger than for other sectors, thus causing an increase in overall price deviance.

40
CONCLUDING REMARKS

The concept of eigenprices is intended to furnish a tool to gauge whether a product or primary factor is over- or under-priced in relation to the market prices of an economy's final deliveries. As such, eigenprices may be looked on as 'true' prices, i.e. prices that would exist in a situation producing the same final flows without imperfections in the markets for commodities or factors. We have seen in this study that the methodology may be useful (1) in studying the historical development of a specific country, and (2) in making international or inter-system comparisons.

When comparing the Netherlands (Tables 35.1 and 35.2) with Hungary, we note that the two sets of eigenprices present radically different patterns. In the case of the Netherlands, deviations from unity are quite small in the domain of commodity prices, while in Hungary these deviations tend to be considerable. This may reflect the fact that Dutch prices are to a large extent determined 'freely' by the forces of demand and supply. Similarly small deviations from unity may well be found for comparable market economies. This is partly confirmed by the pilot study; but it is an area in which further research could usefully be undertaken. In Hungary, where the government still plays a dominant role in the process of price determination independently of market-clearing considerations, eigenprices are clearly seen to deviate from unity quite substantially.

J. Kornai stated that it was the declared intention of the 'third wave of reforms' (1978–82) to 'harden' the financial constraints on state-owned enterprises by imposing a tax subsidy system not easily modifiable by a bargaining process. The 1980 price revision was designed to replace the common 'cost-plus' pricing principle by a price system that would adjust Hungarian domestic prices more readily to prices realized in foreign trade with inconvertible currencies. In official Hungarian terminology, this system is referred to as 'the competitive price system'.[1] We must evidently wait for the publication of the 1981 input–output table before it can be ascertained whether this will result in eigenprices closer to unity (i.e. a lower 'price deviance') than before. (No input–output table is planned for 1980.) It is to be hoped that further research on other East European countries will deepen our understanding of the patterns observed in this exercise.

Two final remarks seem to be called for. First, it should be recalled that the absolute level of eigenprices depends on the method chosen for their 'standardization'. We have here followed the procedure recommended in Part I and the pilot survey, which leaves the total of final demand (i.e. the conventional GNP) invariant. Different types of standardization will lead to a different level of eigenprices, although the relative proportions will remain unaffected. Second, eigenyield and eigenprices are crucially dependent on the interpretations given to such terms as 'labour', 'capital', 'tax', etc., and will also vary with the treatment of social security payments, depreciation, and the like. The allocation of these items to various types of primary inputs must impart a measure of arbitrariness to the calculation, thus tending to vitiate international comparisons. Clearly, whenever two countries fail to record their primary inputs according to a unified definition or breakdown, the comparison between them by the present methods is fraught with considerable danger, and should be undertaken with the utmost care.

Note

1 J. Kornai, 'Comments on the Present State and Prospects of the Hungarian Economic Reform', *Journal of Comparative Economics*, vol. 7, 1983, p. 226.

APPENDIX A
Notation and directory of symbols

Notation

As explained in n. 1 to Chapter 6, we denote row- and column-vectors by using 'acute' and 'grave' accents (´, `) over the corresponding letters respectively; e.g.,

$$[p_1, p_2 \ldots p_n] \equiv \acute{p}$$

$$\begin{pmatrix} z_1 \\ z_2 \\ \cdot \\ \cdot \\ \cdot \\ z_n \end{pmatrix} \equiv \grave{z} \,.$$

This has the advantage of dispensing with bold-faced printing as used in the standard notation and identifies format more clearly than reliance on primes for the transposition of vectors whose original format may be only tacitly assumed or left out of sight altogether. Furthermore, we use a 'circumflex' (ˆ) for diagonal matrices, unaccented capital letters for other matrices, and unaccented lower-case letters (Latin or Greek) for scalars. In particular, I stands for the unit matrix, $\acute{\imath}_r$ and $\grave{\imath}_r$ for its rth row- and column-vectors, and $\acute{\imath}$ and $\grave{\imath}$ for all-unit vectors (with 1 in all positions). The constituent jth column of a matrix, say X, is denoted by $\grave{x}^j$, and its ith row by $\acute{x}_i$, while its total row- and column-sums are denoted by Roman and Greek letters (without affixes) respectively; e.g.,

$$\begin{array}{ll} X\grave{\imath} \equiv \grave{x} & \acute{\imath}X \equiv \acute{\xi} \\ Y\grave{\imath} \equiv \grave{y} & \acute{\imath}Y \equiv \acute{\eta} \quad \text{etc.} \\ W\grave{\imath} \equiv \grave{w} & \acute{\imath}W \equiv \acute{\omega} \end{array}$$

We retain the conventional use of the apostrophe or prime (′) for matrices to denote transposition of rows into columns and *vice versa*, thus enabling us to state the product-transposition theorem in traditional form:

$$(AB)' = B'A'$$

Directory of most frequently occurring symbols

(Numbers in brackets indicate the equation and/or surrounding text where definitions and explanations may be found.)

Some of these symbols are also 'borrowed' to convey different meanings specific to isolated chapters.)

$A = X\hat{z}^{-1}$	$n \times n$ matrix of sectoral ('material') input coefficients (6.6)
$\overline{A\rceil} = (I - A)^{-1}$	the $n \times n$ 'synthesizer' – Leontief inverse of A ((6.7); see Chapter 6, n. 5)
$B = W\hat{z}^{-1}$	$m \times n$ matrix of primary-input (factor-input) coefficients (6.6)
$\acute{b}_r$	row-vector of n direct absorptions (costs) of factor r per unit output of each sector; rth row of B
$C = B\overline{A\rceil}$	$m \times n$ 'cost-matrix' showing in row r the 'full' (direct and indirect) costing of n products in terms of the single factor r (7.4)
$\acute{c}_r$	row-vector of full absorption (cost) of factor r per unit output of each sector ((7.1)–(7.3)); rth row of C
$\acute{c}(f) = \acute{f}C$	row-vector of composite factor-costs of n products when factors are valued at $\acute{f}$ per unit each (7.5)
$F = CN$	$m \times n$ 'cost-norm matrix' ((10.4); see also Chapter 10, n. 2)
$\acute{f}$	dominant left-hand eigenvector of F, defined by $\acute{f}(\phi_* I - F) = \acute{0}$ row-vector of m eigenrentals ((10.3)–(10.4))
$\acute{f}_* = \alpha\acute{f}$	with α chosen to ensure that $\acute{f}_* \grave{w} = \alpha\acute{f}\grave{w} = \phi_* y_0$ row-vector of m standardized eigenrentals (Chapter 12)
ϕ_*	dominant eigenvalue of F, defined by $\acute{f}(\phi_* I - F) = \acute{0}$ or $\lvert\phi_* I - F\rvert = 0$; eigencost ratio; ((10.4), Chapter 10, n. 4, *et seq.*)

$\grave{\imath}, \acute{\imath}$ — all-unit column- and row-vector, taken to be conformable for multiplication with its co-factor in any matrix/vector or vector/vector product and having the effect of simple summation; e.g.,

$$\acute{z}\grave{\imath} = \sum_{r=1}^{n} z_r;\ Y\grave{\imath} = \grave{y}, \acute{\imath}Y = \acute{\eta} = \sum_{r=1}^{n} y_r.$$

$\grave{\imath}_r, \acute{\imath}_r$ — rth column- and row-vector of the unit matrix I, taken to be conformable with its co-factor in any matrix/vector or vector/vector product and having the effect of isolating the rth array or element of that co-factor; e.g.,

$$\acute{z}\grave{\imath}_r = \acute{\imath}_r\grave{z} = z_r; A\,\grave{\imath}_r = \grave{a}_r; \acute{\imath}_r A = \acute{a}^r$$

k — (scalar) number of final use-categories (columns) in the matrix Y, equal to 4 in the second quadrant of tableau (6.1)

$\acute{k}$ — n-dimensional row-vector; absorption of 'capital' services (gross operational surplus) directly used per unit output of each product; short for $\acute{b}_2$, second row of factor-input coefficient matrix B

$\acute{\kappa}$ — $\acute{k}\overline{A}^{\urcorner}$ row-vector of n 'full' capital values of products, defined as direct and indirect absorption (cost) of capital services per unit of each product

$\acute{l}$ — labour services directly used per unit of each of n products; short for $\acute{b}_1$, first row of factor-input coefficient matrix B (Chapter 22)

$\acute{\lambda}$ — $\acute{l}\overline{A}^{\urcorner}$ row-vector of n 'full' labour values of products, defined as direct and indirect absorption (cost) of labour per unit of each product

m — (scalar) number of primary inputs (factors) or rows in third quadrant of tableau (6.1).

$\hat{m}$ — $n \times n$ diagonal matrix of final-use quotas $= \hat{y}\hat{z}^{-1}$ ((8.3) *et seq.*)

$N \quad = \hat{m}\overline{Q}^{\urcorner\prime}R'$
$\quad\;\; = \hat{y}C'\hat{w}^{-1}$ — $n \times m$ matrix of (factor-) norms: ((8.9), (9.3), and Chapter 9, n. 1)

n		(scalar) number of (micro-) sectors in the first quadrant of tableau (6.1); dimension of square matrices, X, A, Q, etc.
$\grave{n}$		column-vector of m factor-norms ((8.7)–(8.8)) and Chapter 8, n. 1)
$\acute{n}(p)$	$= \acute{p}N$	row-vector of m factor-norms when final-use products are valued at $\acute{p}$ per unit each.
P	$= NC$	$n \times n$ 'norm-cost matrix' (10.4)
$\acute{p}$		dominant left-hand eigenvector of P, defined by $\acute{p}(\phi_* I - P) = \acute{0}$; row-vector of n eigen-prices, determined up to a multiplicative constant ((10.3)–(10.4))
$\acute{p}_*$	$= \beta\acute{p}$	with β chosen to ensure that $\acute{p}_* \grave{y} = y_0$; row-vector of n standardized eigenprices per dollar's (lira's) worth (Chapter 12)
$\acute{p}(f)$	$= 1/\phi_* \acute{f} C$	row-vector of total (uniformly marked-up) costs of n products when factors are valued at $\acute{f}$ per unit each ((7.6), (8.10), (10.1–10.4))
Q	$= \hat{z}^{-1} X$	$n \times n$ matrix of sectoral quotas (output allocations to sectors) (8.3)
$Q^{\urcorner}$	$= (I - Q)^{-1}$	Leontief-inverse of Q
$\acute{q}_i$		row-vector of n output-quotas of sector i's product to absorbing sectors (8.2)
R	$= \hat{w}^{-1} W$	$m \times n$ matrix of primary-input (factor-) quotas (9.2)
$\acute{\rho}$	$= \acute{\tau}\hat{z}^{-1}$	row-vector of n surplus/output ratios (Chapter 11, n. 2)
$\acute{\sigma}$	$= \acute{\tau}\hat{\omega}^{-1}$	row-vector of n surplus/value-added ratios (in terms of current prices)
σ_*	$\sigma_* \acute{\imath} = \acute{\tau}_* \hat{\omega}_*^{-1}$ $= 1/\phi_* - 1$	eigenyield; uniform surplus ratio for all sectors (in terms of eigenprices) ((11.1) *et seq* and Chapter 11, n. 2)
$\acute{\tau}$	$= \acute{z} - \acute{\omega} - \acute{\xi}$	row-vector of residual cost-elements or 'surpluses' of n sectors, conventionally identified, but not necessarily identical with indirect taxes net of subsidies
τ	$= \acute{\tau}\grave{\imath} = \sum_{r=1}^{n} \tau_r$	total residual cost-element or 'surplus', conventionally identified, but not necessarily identical with total indirect taxes net of subsidies

$\grave{v}_r$	column-vector of n product-norms based on final-use product r ((8.1)–(8.5))
$\grave{v}(\acute{p}) = \overline{Q}\rceil\hat{m}\grave{p}$	column-vector of n composite product-norms when final uses are valued at $\acute{p}$ per unit each (8.6)
W	$m \times n$ matrix of primary-input (factor-) flows; third quadrant of tableau (6.1) excluding $\acute{\tau}$-row
$\grave{w}$	column-vector of m primary-inputs (factors) used; row-sums of third quadrant of tableau (6.1) excluding τ
$\acute{\omega}$	row-vector of n total primary-input (factor-) flows into production sectors; column-sums of third quadrant of tableau (6.1) excluding $\acute{\tau}$-row
X	$n \times n$ matrix of intersectoral flows evaluated in current prices; first quadrant of tableau (6.1)
$\grave{x} = X\grave{\imath}$	column-vector of n sector outputs for intermediate use; row-sums of first quadrant of tableau (6.1)
$\acute{\xi} = \acute{\imath}X$	row-vector of n total sectoral ('non-factor') inputs; column-sums of first quadrant of tableau (6.1)
Y	$n \times k$ matrix of 'yields' (supplies for k final uses); second quadrant of tableau (6.1)
$\grave{y} = \grave{z} - \grave{x} = Y'\grave{\imath}$	column-vector of total final uses (evaluated in current prices) supplied by n production sectors; row-sums of second quadrant of tableau (6.1)
$y_0 = \acute{\imath}\grave{y} = \sum_{r=1}^{n} y_r$	GNP (-surrogate) in current prices
$y_* = \acute{\imath}\grave{y}_* = y_0$	'Standard GNP'; GNP (-surrogate) in standardized eigenprices, by definition equal to y_0 (Chapter 12)
$\grave{y}_* = \hat{p}_*\grave{y}$	column-vector of n total final uses ('yields') valued in standardized eigenprices
$\acute{\eta} = \acute{\imath}Y$	row-vector of k final uses in current prices; column-sums of second quadrant of tableau (6.1)

$\acute{z}$	$= \grave{x} + \grave{y}$ $= \grave{\xi} + \grave{\omega} + \grave{\tau}$	column-vector of n total sectoral outputs (= inputs + surplus); row-sums of first plus second quadrants of tableau (6.1), by assumption equal to column-sums of first plus third quadrants of tableau (6.1)

APPENDIX B
Eigenprices and cost-values

Since eigenprices are constructed with the special object of avoiding the twin defects of 'factor-monomania' and 'cost-fetishism', which – in my submission – distort traditional model prices of a diagnostic nature, it is of particular importance to measure and analyse their deviations from such prices in the context of an empirical study. The computation by which eigenprices are obtained (Chapters 6–10) throws up a number of 'cost-fetishist' and 'monomaniac' values as intermediate steps in the procedure, which are therefore readily available for the purpose in hand.[1]

Table B1 compares the Marxian labour-values λ with eigenprices p_* for our nine macro-sectors in five countries, and analyses the multiplicative correction-factor $\iota = p_*/\lambda$ ('inflator'), which provides the link, and factorizes into the part played by the admission of 'co-factors' other than labour (cofactor-inflator ι_1) and the part played by influences from the demand-side (use-value inflator ι_2). The first of these components defines the effect of eliminating 'monomania', while the second measures that of amending 'cost-fetishism' by admitting use-value alongside costs into value formation.

The table makes it clear that the effects of eliminating monomania (ι_1) are nearly everywhere considerably stronger than those of correcting for cost-fetishism (ι_2), with the latter being virtually of uniform size in all the sectors of a given country. This is indeed to be expected whenever the standardized eigenrentals f_*^1, f_*^2 differ only marginally from unity, thus making eigenprices:

$$\acute{p}_* = \frac{1}{\pi} \acute{f}_* C$$

virtually equal to full total factor costs:

$$\acute{\lambda} + \acute{\kappa} = \acute{\imath} C.$$

As a result the ratio ι_2 becomes nearly identical with $1/\pi$ throughout the system.

Table B *Eigenprices and cost-values compared*

		A	B	C	D	E	F	G	H	I
Czechoslovakia 1973										
Labour value	λ	0.589	0.387	0.386	0.232	0.348	0.304	0.358	0.389	0.424
'Capital value'	κ	0.130	0.373	0.164	0.341	0.341	0.255	0.296	0.309	0.277
Cofactor inflator	ι_1	1.221	1.964	1.425	2.470	1.980	1.839	1.827	1.794	1.653
Use-value inflator	ι_2	1.527	1.531	1.531	1.532	1.533	1.531	1.532	1.530	1.531
Eigenprice	p_*	1.098	1.164	0.842	0.878	1.056	0.856	1.002	1.068	1.073
W. Germany 1970										
Labour value	λ	0.285	0.499	0.360	0.525	0.585	0.561	0.523	0.542	0.523
'Capital value'	κ	0.701	0.327	0.465	0.395	0.326	0.342	0.374	0.336	0.397
Cofactor inflator	ι_1	3.460	1.655	2.292	1.752	1.557	1.610	1.715	1.620	1.759
Use-value inflator	ι_2	1.106	1.110	1.108	1.108	1.110	1.109	1.108	1.108	1.109
Eigenprice	p_*	1.091	0.917	0.914	1.019	1.011	1.002	0.994	0.973	1.020
Japan 1970										
Labour value	λ	0.195	0.438	0.273	0.322	0.427	0.465	0.416	0.447	0.429
'Capital value'	κ	0.781	0.497	0.573	0.500	0.481	0.453	0.480	0.465	0.487
Cofactor inflator	ι_1	5.005	2.135	3.099	2.553	2.126	1.974	2.154	2.040	2.135
Use-value inflator	ι_2	1.104	1.104	1.104	1.105	1.105	1.105	1.104	1.104	1.104
Eigenprice	p_*	1.077	1.032	0.934	0.908	1.003	1.104	0.989	1.007	1.011
United Kingdom 1972										
Labour value	λ	0.407	0.682	0.451	0.429	0.619	0.558	0.523	0.560	0.595
'Capital value'	κ	0.492	0.215	0.296	0.218	0.164	0.164	0.216	0.304	0.285
Cofactor inflator	ι_1	2.209	1.315	1.656	1.508	1.265	1.294	1.413	1.543	1.479
Use-value inflator	ι_2	1.206	1.203	1.205	1.206	1.204	1.205	1.206	1.205	1.206
Eigenprice	p_*	1.084	1.079	0.900	0.780	0.943	0.870	0.891	1.041	1.061

USSR 1972										
Labour value	λ	0.687	0.365	0.494	0.299	0.427	0.367	0.429	0.552	0.452
'Capital value'	κ	0.288	0.576	0.366	0.508	0.490	0.347	0.425	0.402	0.525
Cofactor inflator	ι_1**	1.419	2.578	1.741	2.699	2.148	1.946	1.991	1.728	2.162
Use-value inflator	ι_2**	1.125	1.122	1.124	1.123	1.123	1.124	1.123	1.125	1.123
Eigenprice	p_*	1.097	1.056	0.967	0.906	1.030	0.803	0.959	1.073	1.097

Notes

The nine sectors retain the meaning of Tables 29.3 and 31.1, i.e.
A = Agriculture, fishing and forestry; B = Mining, quarrying, fuel extractions; C = Food, drink, and tobacco; D = Chemicals, plastics, rubber, etc.; E = Metals and engineering; F = Textiles, leather, and clothing; G = Other manufacturing; H = Construction; I = Utilities, transport, trade, and services.

All values are pure numbers (£ per £).

Labour- and 'capital'-values are defined in (7.3), (22.1), and Chapter 22 as $\acute{\lambda} = \acute{l}\overline{A}|$ and $\acute{\kappa} = \acute{k}\overline{A}|$, so that the first two rows above for each country reproduce the cost-matrix $C(= B\overline{A}|)$; see (7.4). The cofactor-inflator ι_1 = coefficient by which labour-value λ must be multipled to give total factor-cost of each product; i.e., $\iota_1 = 1 + \kappa/\lambda$, such that $\kappa + \lambda = \lambda\iota_1$.

The use-value-inflator ι_2 = coefficient by which total factor-cost of each product must be multiplied to give standardized eigenprice, i.e. $\iota_2 = [(1 + \kappa_*\lambda_*)/(1 + \kappa/\lambda)]\ f_*$, such that $p_* = \lambda\iota_1\iota_2$.

The product of the two inflators $\iota_1\iota_2$ thus measures the 'labour-inflator' ι by which labour-value must be multiplied to give the standardized eigenprice of each product, i.e. $p_* = \lambda\iota$.

It should be noted that the table is based solely on computations on 'preconsolidated' data, i.e. on input–output tables condensed into the same nine macro-sectors in each country.

Note

1 Similar computations for Austria and Hungary, though without direct comparisons with eigenprices, are presented in a particularly valuable monograph by G. Fink, *Preisverzerrungen und Unterschiede in der Produktionsstruktur zwischen Österreich und Ungarn* (Springer-Verlag, Vienna New York, 1981), which also explains derivation and rationale in a most illuminating way. For a shortened version see also Gerhard Fink, 'Price Distortions in the Austrian and in the Hungarian Economy', *Zeitschrift für National-ökonomie*, vol. 41, 1981, pp. 111–32.

APPENDIX C

The current and standardized eigen-structure of the United Kingdom in 1972

As an illustration of the computations undertaken on the original 60-sector data for the United Kingdom (and other fully disaggregated input–output tables whose articulation is shown in Table 29.1), we present here the data and results of the pre-consolidation exercise which condensed all country tables into the nine 'macro-sectors' defined in tables 29.3, 31.1 and B1. The eigenprices emerging from this are of course the 'macro-prices' quoted in brackets in Table 29.3, which differ from the proper 'micro-prices' discussed in the other text tables, owing to inevitable aggregation errors. The use of the latter would have necessitated a transformation in which the flows from any given production sector were subjected to *differential* revaluation according to their sectors of destination, to take account of the different 'micro-mixes' making up these flows. The use of macro-prices, however, though tainted by aggregation errors, allows the transformation procedures and results to be shown up in a more transparent way.

Table C presents the current-price structure in the upper tableau (above the middle line) and transforms this into the 'standard structure' (i.e. the same structure in terms of standard eigenprices) in the lower tableau, as indicated by the asterisked subscripts on the left-hand margin. Only the first quadrant (*A* to *I*), the factor-inputs *W*, and the total output column *z* are directly taken from the data (in consolidated form). The final-demand column *y* is supplied by the author as the residual between total output *z* and total sectoral deliveries *x*, and the surplus-row τ as the residual within value added (i.e. $z - \omega - \xi$). The last column of the upper tableau shows the standardized macro-eigenprices p_* and eigenrentals f_* by which the corresponding rows are multiplied (revalued) to give the lower tableau. The row-totals of the

Table C *Preconsolidated flows in the United Kingdom (1972) in current- and eigenprices (£ million)*

	A	B	C	D	E	F	G	H	I	x	y	z	p_*
A	816	1	1387	8	0	45	21	0	42	2,320	1,381	3,701	1.0838
B	24	267	80	176	331	8	40	943	578	2,447	591	3,038	1.0793
C	578	2	880	77	3	5	11	2	121	1,679	5,954	7,633	0.9002
D	260	180	203	1474	804	252	260	183	714	4,330	2,655	6,985	0.7800
E	56	321	244	288	7,593	86	174	897	1,110	10,769	11,281	22,050	0.9428
F	19	12	5	50	60	1394	72	4	251	1,867	2,838	4,705	0.8697
G	34	70	266	139	273	69	903	428	1,266	3,448	1,978	5,426	0.8910
H	54	78	19	11	121	8	10	854	192	1,347	6,725	8,072	1.0414
I	294	560	1361	1096	2,242	539	791	430	4,145	11,458	32,462	43,920	1.0606
ξ	2135	1490	4445	3319	11,427	2407	2282	3741	8,420	39,666	65,865	105,531	f_*
W_1	516	1192	1228	1270	6,799	1299	1598	2282	21,299	37,483			1.0045
W_2	1066	302	760	736	1,381	278	631	1591	10,458	17,203			1.0114
ω	1582	1494	1988	2006	8,180	1577	2229	3873	31,757	54,686			
τ	−16	54	1200	1660	2,443	721	915	458	3,743	11,179			
z	3701	3038	7633	6985	22,050	4705	5426	8072	43,920	105,531			
$\acute{\sigma}$ $(\equiv \tau/\omega)$	−0.010	0.036	0.604	0.828	0.299	0.457	0.410	0.142	0.118	0.204			
A_*	884	1	1503	9	0	49	23	0	46	2,514	1,497	4,011	
B_*	26	288	86	190	357	9	43	1018	624	2,641	638	3,279	
C_*	520	2	792	69	3	5	10	2	109	1,511	5,360	6,871	
D_*	203	140	158	1150	627	197	203	143	557	3,377	2,071	5,448	
E_*	53	303	230	272	7,159	81	164	846	1,047	10,153	10,636	20,789	
F_*	17	10	4	43	52	1212	63	3	218	1,624	2,468	4,092	
G_*	30	62	237	124	243	61	805	381	1,128	3,072	1,762	4,834	

H_*	56	81	20	11	126	18	10	1889	200	1,403	7,003	8,406
I_*	312	594	1443	1162	2,378	572	839	456	4,396	12,152	34,430	46,582
ξ_*	2101	1481	4473	3030	10,945	2194	2160	3738	8,325	38,447	65,865	104,312
W_1^*	518	1197	1234	1276	6,830	1305	1605	2292	21,395	37,652		
W_2^*	1078	305	769	744	1,397	281	638	1609	10,577	17,399		
ω_*	1596	1502	2003	2020	8,227	1586	2243	3901	31,972	55,051		
τ_*	314	296	395	398	1,617	312	432	767	6,285	10,814		
z_*	4011	3279	6871	5448	20,789	4092	4835	8406	46,582	104,312		
$\sigma_*(\equiv \tau_*/\omega_*)$	0.197	0.197	0.197	0.197	0.197	0.197	0.193	0.197	0.197	0.196		

latter are then carried over into the penultimate row z_* and the residual eigensurplus τ_* is ascertained by subtraction $(z_* - \omega_* - \xi_*)$.

The crucial effect aimed at by the transformation is clearly visible from a comparison of the last rows of each tableau, in which the surplus-margin $\sigma(= \tau/\omega)$ is shown: this is highly variable from one sector to another in terms of current prices, ranging from -1 to nearly 83 per cent, but reduces to the single ratio σ_* (19.7 per cent) which is uniform (but for rounding errors) for all sectors. The 'standardized' scaling of eigenprices has moreover ensured that our proxy for the GNP (sum of y-column) remains invariant to the transformation at £65,865 million. Readers will recall that this differs considerably from the GNP of the official national accounts by virtue of the exclusion of factor-services directly absorbed in final uses, the special treatment of imports, and other discrepancies between input–output and national accounts statistics.

Index

Subject headings are in italics, proper-names without emphasis unless qualifying as subjects (e.g. *Marx, Pareto*)

References are to pages and distinguished as follows:

ack	Acknowledgment
bbg	Bibliographic reference
qtd	Quotation

Entries in quotes (' ') refer to terms coined by the author, not in common use, or commonly used in a non-specific sense.

Abouchar, A. bbg 16n, 95n
'Accent notation' vi, 27n
Adjusted factor-costs (Bergson) 7, 9
Aggregation (of sectors) 111, 113–15, 152–6
  'pre-consolidation' 113–14
  'post-consolidation' 113–14, 122
  aggregation errors 114–15
  condensation ratio 114
Artis, M. bbg 65n
Augmentation (of matrices and vectors) 67, 68, 73
Augustinovics, M. bbg 34n

Bailing out, possibility of (influence on surplus) 152
Bánhidi, F. ack 132
Basic scheme, Basic tableau 25, 26
Becker, A. S. 10n
Bergson, A. 7, 9, bbg 10n, 49n
Black box 3, 4
Bródy, A. ack 132, bbg 34n, 43n, 78n
Brus, W. bbg 132n, qtd 149n

Capacity 72
  'capacity-cost' 70, 71
  'capacity-cost saving' 70
  'capacity-equivalent' 70
  'capacity-product' 72
Capital
  'capital-cost' 14
  'capital monomania' 14
  'capital-value' 30, 169, 170
  constant (Marxian) 92
  variable (Marxian) 92
Carpenter, C. ack vii, 108n
Carter, A. P. bbg 34n
Champernowne, D. G. bbg 78n
Circulation
  'cost-generating' 52–3
  'norm-generating' 36–9, 52–3
'Cloning'
  'price-cloning' 9
Coefficients
  coefficient matrices 26
  consumption 92
  input 26, 33
  Leontief 73, 96
Comparability, Comparison 4–5, 6
Competitiveness 117
Complementarity (between sectors in pricing) 143
Composite costs 16, 30
Composite norms 33

'Conjugate' duality (linear programming) 61, 62n, 64
Condensation, see Aggregation
condensation ratio 114
Consolidation, see Aggregation
'pre-consolidation' 113–14
'post-consolidation' 113–14, 122
'Consumer-orientation' (effect on pricing) 128
Cost 4, 29
adjusted factor 7, 9
'composite costs' 16, 30
cost-efficiency, cost-effectiveness 45, 97, 117, 119, 129
'cost-fetishism' 4, 7, 12–16, 32, 85, 169
'cost-matrix' 29
'cost-monomania' 29
'cost-norm matrix' 42, 43n, 57, 94
'cost-prices' 61
'cost-standard' 29
cost valuations, cost values 15–16, 29, 30, 169
cost/turnover ratio, cost-ratio 16, 24, 93
full costs, full-cost pricing 16, 29, 30, 57, 61
'full-price costing' 32
'release-costs' 72
Cross-section analysis 109–28
Cyclical movements (Netherlands) 145
Csikós-Nagy, B. bbg 124n

de Galan, C. bbg 136n
'Diagnostic' prices' 9, 98–9
Dietzenbacher, E. ack vii, 108n, 132
Dimension 12–13, 17n, 27n, 48–9
'dimensional incoherence' 13
'dimensional balance' 48–9
see also 'lira', 'perun'
Dixit, A. bbg 65n, 102
Dyadic matrices 58, 86

Eckaus, R. S. bbg 88n
Eigencost 44
eigencost ratio 44–5, 57, 59, 77, 93, 96, 102, 114
generation of 52–4
partial 80–1, 90
Eigenprice vi, 59n, 22–3, 101, 161–2
absolute level 162
caveat 23, 101–3, 162
definition 41–3, 44–7, 58–9, 70–4, 93, 96–7
departure from current prices 121–3, 125
empirical tests 107–62
external ('foreign trade-geared') 80–1
generation 52–3
'partial eigenprices' 79–81, 89–90, 94–5
pre-tax and post-tax 89, 90
scaling 50–1
sensitivity to current pricing of flows 111, 160
sensitivity to aggregation 113–15, 145, 160
sensitivity to treatment of imports 110–11
sensitivity to economic system 130–1
skewness of distribution 127
standardized 50, 162
terminology 43n
uses 23, 87, 98–100
Eigenratios
structural 125–6
performance *see* eigencost ratio, eigenyield
Eigenrentals 64, 99, 159
partial 81, 90
'Eigensurplus' 45–7, 130
'eigensurplus ratio' (= 'eigenyield') 23, 44–7, 58, 70, 74, 96–7, 130
'Eigenvalues'
absolute 'eigenvalues' 51
'Eigenyield' (= 'eigensurplus ratio') 23, 44–7, 58, 70, 74, 96–7, 130
empirical findings 117, 145
invariance to current prices 49
'pre-tax eigenyield' 46
Empirical tests 107–62
cross-section analysis (pilot survey) 107–28
Hungary 146–60
Netherlands 133–45
time-series analysis 129–62
Errors in earlier survey 109–10, 112n
Expenditure function (= 'minimum expenditure function') 64, 69
Exploitation
rate of (Marxian) 45, 92

Factor
'factor-base' 47, 153–4
factor cost *see separate entry*
'factor-free' models 76–8
'factor-liras' 13
'factor-norms' 20, 30, 35–6, 49
generation of 38–9
'factor-quotas' 33, 57
factor-rentals (-prices) 61, 64
factor substitution 63
'factor-valuation matrix' 58
Factor-cost 8
adjusted (Bergson) 7, 9
'composite factor-cost' 15
'single-factor' cost 34
Feedback
feedback effects (of prices on quantities) 26
'feedback-free' models 57–62
Fetishism
'cost-fetishism' 3, 7, 12, 130
'use-fetishism' 18, 32, 130
Fink, G. bbg 132n, 172n
Fortuyn, W. S. P. 136n
'Functional' prices 9, 129

Gerschenkron, A. 10n
Gilbert (Kravis–Gilbert method) 9
GNP (Gross National Product) and surrogate 28n
Gomulka, S. ack vii
'Goods-lira' 12–13, 17n
Gorman, T. ack vii, 62n, bbg 65n
'Grafting' ('price-grafting') 8–9, 120

Hague, Sir Douglas bbg 124n
Hare, P. bbg 149n
Hejl, L. bbg 78n
Hessian (matrix) 67, 69, 74
bordered 67, 69
bordered sub- 73
Heston, A. bbg 11n
Hewett, E. A. bbg 149n
Heymann, H. Jr. bbg 10n
Hodgman, D. bbg 10n
Hoeffding, O. bbg 10n
Holzman, F. D. bbg 10n
Hungary 131, 146–60
influence of market mechanism 148
NEM (New Economic Mechanism) 131, 147–8
terms of trade 148

ICP (International Comparison Project) 8, 9
IMF (International Monetary Fund) bbg 132n, 149n
'Import-value' 30
Imports (statistical treatment) 110–12
Input–Output
'Articulation' 117
Disaggregation of sectors 111–12
Input-coefficients 26, 33
'Input-planning/Output-pricing' 62n, 152
Quadrants 27n, 76
Pricing conventions 110–12
Statistical problems 107–12
Units of observation 111
Investment goods (pricing) 121–2

Jasny, N. bbg 10n
Joint production 27n

Kenessy, Z. bbg 11n
Kornai, J. 161–2, bbg 132n, 148–9n
Kravis, I. (Kravis–Gilbert method) 8–9, bbg 11n
Kýn, O. bbg 78n

Labour-costs
direct 13–14, 29
full 29, 169–72
indirect 13–14, 29
Labour-hours (Marxian units) 91
Labour-intensity (effect on pricing) 128
'Labour-monomania' 12
Labour-values 12, 169–72
Marxian 9, 12, 29, 91–5
definition 'by imputation' and 'by alienation' 91–3
Lagrangean methods 64, 66
'Land-values' 30
Laski, K. ack vii
League tables 8–9
Leontief, Wassily 7
closed Leontief model 78n
Leontief-Inverse (matrix) 28n, 57
'Square Table' 7, 76
see also Input–Output
Limitational (of production function) 26
'Lin' (abbreviation for Leontief-Inverse matrix) 28n

Linear programming 60–2
'Lira' 27n
'factor-lira' (flr) 13, 17n
'goods-lira' (glr) 13, 17n
Little, I. M. D.: bbg 51n
Little–Mirrlees (OECD) method of project appraisal 82–8

'Macro-sectors' 113–14, 152
see also Aggregation
Malinvaud, E. 102
Mapping 34, 36, 42, 43
'reflexive mapping' 42
see also Transformation
Marginal analysis 66–75
marginal cost 59, 62, 69, 71
marginal productivity 61, 68
Mark-up 24
see also Eigensurplus, Eigenyield, VAT-coefficient
'Marketing problem' (linear programming) 60
Marx, K. bbg 21n
Marxian labour-values 9, 29, 91–5
Marxism 12
'Material-intensity' (effect on pricing) 128
Maximum-value function 66, 68
Mazzarino, G. ack vii, 108n
Menger, N. bbg 78n
'Micro-sectors' 113–14, 122
see also Aggregation
Mihályi, P. bbg 149n
'Minimal expenditure function' 64, 69
Mirrlees, J. A. ack vii, bbg 51n
Little–Mirrlees (OECD) method of project appraisal 82–8
Molnár, Gy. ack 132
'Monomania' 7, 12, 32
'capital monomania' 14
'cost monomania' 12, 15, 85, 169
'norm monomania' 20
'use monomania' 18
Morishima, M. ack vii, 7, bbg 43n
MPS (Material Product System) 130

Netherlands 133–45
Nimitz, N. bbg 10n
Nobay, R. bbg 65n
Non-linearity (in functions) 63, 73, 74
'Norms' ('use-norms') 4, 15, 18–21, 30–9, 85, 93–4
'commodity norms' 18
'composite norms' 33
'cost-norm matrix' 42
'factor-norms' 30–2, 38–9
generation of 'norms' 36–9
'norm-cost matrix' 42, 58
'norming circulation' 36–9, 52–3
'norm matrix' 33–5, 73–4, 94
'single-yield factor norms' 34
Notation 27n, 31n, 163–8
'accent notation' vi, 27n, 163
'subscript–superscript notation' 27n, 31n
Nove, A. ack 31n

OECD shadow prices (Little–Mirrlees method of project appraisal) 82–8
Optimization 101
Pareto optima 65
'Output-planning/input-pricing' 62n

Pareto (optimization) 65, 101
'Perun' 17n
'Pluralism' (in factor-base) 12, 16
Prices
border-prices (Little–Mirrlees, OECD method) 82–8
'border-price content' 85, 88n
channel-prices (two-channel prices etc.) 77
consumer 121–2, 159
'current pricing' 118–23
'diagnostic prices' 9, 77, 129
'full-cost pricing' 29–31, 161
'functional prices' 9, 129
investment 121–2
N-income 77
'price-cloning' 9
'price-grafting' 8–9, 120
'price-deviance', *see separate entry*
price-discrimination 13, 111
'price-pruning' 7
pricing conventions (input–output) 111–12
production (Marxian) 77
'shadow-prices' *see* border prices
'under-pricing' and 'over-pricing' 117–23, 127–8, 159
world (for international comparison) 8
'Price-deviance' 116, 116n, 160
definition 116n
Prime costs ('global') 92

'PRM' ('principle of reciprocal marginality') 58, 59, 62–75, 78
Production
joint 27n
production-prices (Marxian) 77
'production problem' (linear programming) 60
Product, Productivity
'capacity-product' 72
marginal physical product 58, 67
marginal revenue productivity 21, 58, 61
'release productivity' 71
Profit (in CMEA) 120
Profit-rate 30
'Pruning', see 'price-pruning'

'Quasi-competitive prices' 62
'Quotas' 57
'factor-quotas' 33, 57
'final-use quotas' 33
'output-quotas' 32, 57

Radice, H. bbg 149n
'Realistic prices' (linear programming) 60
'Reciprocal Marginality' (Principle of, PRM) 58, 59, 62–75, 78
'Release-costs', 'release-productivities' 73
Rentals (factor-prices)
'external rentals' 81
Representative commodity (Sraffa) 77
Revenue productivity (marginal) 21, 58, 61
Rosenstein-Rodan, N. bbg 88n

Samuelson, P. A. ack vii, 11n
Scaling
of eigenprices 50–1, 81, 90
scaling factor 51
Scott, M. FG. ack vii, 49n
Second-order conditions (in optimization) 75n
Sector definitions
branch-type and administrative-type 150–1
see also Aggregation and *Input–Output,* unit of observation
Sekerka, B. bbg 78n
Seton, F. bbg 11n, 16n, ack 32, bbg 43n, 51n, 87n, 95n, 112n, 132n

Shadow prices, see Prices, border
SNA (System of National Accounts) 130
'Square Table' (Input–Output Table) 7
Sraffa, P. ack 7, bbg 78n
'Standardization' (of eigenprices), see Scaling
Steenge, A. E. 107, ack vii
Stellingwerff, J. ack 132
'Subscript–superscript notation' 25, 27n
Subsistence-wage, -basket 87
Summers, R. bbg 10n
'Supply problem' (linear programming) 61
Surplus-rate (rate of surplus) 76
Surplus 25, 76
Marxian 92
operational (in CMEA) 120
Swain, N. bbg 149n
'Synthesizer', 'Synthesization' 29, 92
Systemic classification (of 'eigenprice' structure) 130–1
Systemic merit (Bergson) 45
Szakolcsai, Gy. ack vii, 132, bbg 124n

'Take-over problem' (linear programming) 61
Tax 25, 47
direct and indirect taxes 102
pre-tax and post-tax eigenprices 89, 159
value-added tax (VAT) coefficient 44
Time-series analysis 129–62
Tradable and Non-tradable goods (in calculation of shadow prices) 83–5
Trade-terms (terms of trade)
of sectors 128
Hungary 148
Transformation, see also Mapping 41, 50
'downstream transformation' 34–5, 64, 68, 70, 80, 91
'reflexive transformation' (mapping) 42, 64, 70
'upstream transformation' 34–5, 64, 66, 69, 70, 80
'transformation function' 63, 67

United Kingdom (input–output in

current- and eigen-prices, pre-consolidated for 1972) 173–5
Use, usefulness, utility (as factor in value-formation) 3–4, 18
'use-fetishism' 18–21
'use-norms' ('norms') 35–9, 93
Utilization (of resources) 101–2

'Valuation-base' 76
'Valuation matrices' 97n
Value v, 3, 5
'capital-, import-, land-value' 30
labour-value 9, 12, 30
value-in-use (Marx) 18
VAT (Value-added tax) coefficient 44, 96–7
von Neumann, J. 77, bbg 78n
Wage-rental ratio 122
Wassily (= Leontief, W.) 7
Wiles, P. J. D. vii, bbg 10n
Windmuller, J. P. bbg 136n
World prices (for international comparison) 8

'Yield' 25
'single-yield norms' 34
'yield-norms' 57
'yield-products', 'yield-productivities' 35–6, 57

ZWO (Netherlands Organisation for the Advancement of Pure Research) ack 132